THE STATE OF WATER

THE STATE OF
WATER

Understanding California's Most Precious Resource

written and illustrated by
OBI KAUFMANN

Heyday, Berkeley, California

Library of Congress Cataloging-in-Publication Data

Names: Kaufmann, Obi, author.
Title: The state of water : understanding California's most precious
  resource / Obi Kaufmann.
Description: Berkeley, California : Heyday, 2019. | Includes bibliographical
  references.
Identifiers: LCCN 2018047383 (print) | LCCN 2018060603 (ebook) | ISBN
  9781597144766 (E-book) | ISBN 9781597144698 (pbk.)
Subjects: LCSH: Water-supply--California. | Water use--California. |
  Water conservation--California. | Water resources development--California.
Classification: LCC TD224.C3 (ebook) | LCC TD224.C3 K353 2019 (print)
  | DDC 333.91009794--dc23
LC record available at https://lccn.loc.gov/2018047383

Cover Design: Ashley Ingram
Interior Design: Obi Kaufmann and Ashley Ingram

Published by Heyday
P.O. Box 9145, Berkeley, California 94709
(510) 549-3564
www.heydaybooks.com

Printed in East Peoria, Illinois, by Versa Press, Inc.

10 9 8 7 6 5 4 3 2 1

To all the children in my family:
Sophia, Finn, Olive, Zoe, Owen, Austin,
Vander, Olivia, Ruby, and Emilia

American white Pelican
Pelecanus erythrorhynchos

Lahontan cutthroat trout
Oncorhynchus clarkii henshawi

"We don't govern water. Water governs us."

—Kalahari proverb[1]

We carry into our future at least as many responsibilities as we do rights.

This is our charge.

We have the right to extract, but we have the responsibility to replenish.

We have the right to develop, but we have the responsibility to restore.

We have the right to inhabit, but we have the responsibility to set aside.

Stewardship is the active management of leaving the more-than-human world to its own functioning devices.

CONTENTS

Part four: A Moment of Restoration

Part five: Patterns in Conservation

INTRODUCTION

01.a The State of Water

Most of California, especially the parts where most of the people live, is truly arid. Water is life, and the idea that there is not enough of it to go around is potentially the most divisive splintering agent to this or any society whose environment cannot support agriculture without irrigation.[1] It is not just that water security, as an abstract yet all-encompassing priority, is or is not capable of dividing or of ripping apart communities in California on whatever scale, but it is the willingness of political and business entities to exploit that potential that represents the largest threat to our unity and civility.

Unity is at the core of my presentation. There is only one California to serve. If this book carries a political agenda, it is to point out our agreements over our differences. Water culture in California is built as much on tradition as it is on infrastructure. Deconstructing that tradition is not in the scope of this presentation. The disposition of this book is pragmatic, not idealistic. I assume that the answers to the dilemmas that concern us—water security for all, our climate future, preserving our biodiversity, and honoring our history of agriculture and the culture that it supports—are not only out there, but easier, or at least less painful than we might suppose. The job of this book is to examine and present the large water systems of California, and to further argue the case for water conservation, as it is the official policy of the state. But this is not a book on public policy. I don't spend too much time talking about groundwater, as my main scope of interest is surface water and how systems of rivers and aqueducts impact habitat for wildlife. My bias is to surface water solutions and systems, as that is my focus as a naturalist, a painter, and a lover of the natural world of California.

This book is a cursory survey, a thumbnail view of the ecological reality of our water future by examining the systems of our water past. It is a tall order and I am happy to wade out into the contentious flood. I don't dwell on speculative or emerging technological solutions for water use. I also don't delve too much into water rights and seniority. This is not a work of history. Despite its dependence on data-driven maps and statistics, this is as much a work of philosophy as it is a work of systems thinking in the context of California water. In writing this book, I serve you, my community, and thereby myself in a calm circle of understanding. I'm not banging my fist on the table. Those days are done.

This is not a work of pure geographic literacy. I am not pretending to describe this incredibly complex system dispassionately; in fact it doesn't even interest me to do so. If I were interested in a purely scientific vision, void of passion and perspective—in just another California water study (and plenty of them do already exist)—I would have chosen a different profession. Alas, I am the same artist-naturalist that painted the *California Field Atlas* and I maintain that my vision—a vision that always begins with data-driven inspiration—is human, biased, nuanced, and at times messy. I let a flowery language of poetry infiltrate this book on many levels.

This book is a specific kind of examination into the California waterscape. It is an account of my own journey to understand it and the way it serves and perhaps doesn't serve us and the natural world, now and going into the future. I take exceptional license, always, and have shielded myself by calling my work the work of an artist. Although this work resembles a piece of journalism or maybe even a submission of scientific merit, it is neither. I am a naturalist (a student of natural history) and I present this work as a journal of my investigation, weighted and probably even encumbered by and with my perspective.

Consumnes River

A book of poetry

Human meaning is not the same as truth. Truth is measured in data. Meaning is the product of examination and derivation through a narrative experience. Meaning and truth are investigable through art and science, respectively. Throughout this book, I break with the theme of water analysis to present several moments of resonance, inspired encapsulations accompanied by my wildlife renderings. I've named each poem-like piece after the animal it juxtaposes on the page, only sometimes attached to the content of the section, exploring the spirit of the work and my appreciation of and my bewilderment by the world that is California water.

The Great Blue Heron

The legacy of one hundred thousand years of storytelling is reflected in both our individual minds and the collective mind we each tap whenever we speak, create, and love. Our society is built on stories. A story, either composed of words or pictorially rendered in art, transmits apprehensible information. A flower well rendered in paint, for example, transmits viable immediate beauty, everything a human could know, or at least needs to know, to identify and appreciate the reality of that flower on some, almost metabolic level—something core revealed and celebrated, a communion and an atonement with that flower's world. We change the story, we change the world. Depending on how we fare in the coming, inevitable paradigm shift, we will be charting a course not only of our continued human residency here over the next one hundred or five hundred years, but over the next ten thousand years. Let's go ahead and trust each other enough to begin that conversation.

Great Blue heron
Ardea herodias

01.b Perspective

How humans use water in California can be terribly confusing, as water exists in a labyrinth of convoluted allocations that are, certainly, intentionally circuitous. What I thought was going to be an essay turned into this reference manual. While there may be nothing straightforward about California water, I set about to see how simply I could describe it. I found that by describing the massive system that is California water, or more specifically, the monumentally complex infrastructure of human control and management of California water, ethical questions inevitably arose. How do we preserve California's endangered aquatic biodiversity in the face of climate change and an ever-growing population? If we choose to keep going the way we've always gone, setting the economic doctrine of infinite growth as our singular guiding light, are we making a system that is more resilient or are we just putting off the harder decisions for another day? How can infinite growth occur in a finite system of resources? We've done exceptionally well with broadening the parameters of those limited systems, but if the system breaks, shouldn't we care that we are speeding toward a disaster of our own making?

I constructed nine maps—nine water situations that together present the most concise and yet complete story of historical and present-day water use in California. More than any kind of policy answers, this book reflects an attitude that leans toward hope and not despair. This book is a reference compilation of figures and maps that presumes the answer to our water worries exists as a compromise between powers and interests.

the lack of rain defines all

The mapping begins with an overview, an introduction to the wild and the artificial interface of infrastructure and our state's legacy of wild rivers and water bodies, some of which (Tulare Lake and Owens Lake) did not survive the first half of the twentieth century. In the second map, I quote the Wild and Scenic Rivers Act as our highest ideal, however compromised it might be in its limited inventory. In the third map, I end the first part with an extensive yet incomplete rundown of California's water storage and conveyance systems. Moving to northern rivers and the San Joaquin with the three maps in the next section, I explore the theme of the salmon as the central, defining idea. I use the salmon as a symbol to probe what we have lost and as the ethical bedrock of the conservation movement. I discuss the Sacramento River, and how the dangerous, aging infrastructure of its tributaries obstructs efforts for salmon populations to regain a foothold and what implications this has for the ecosystem at large. I examine the San Joaquin River Restoration Project in central California and how because of its efforts, we witnessed spring-run Chinook salmon spawn south of Friant Dam for the first time in sixty years. I close the section looking north, with a celebration of the pending removal of four dams on the Klamath River and the implications for the recovery of salmon populations. Moving to the south in the next section, I call the Salton Sea our state's number-one mess—our single most costly and important remediation emergency—before moving to present the Colorado River and some of the major policies that govern its straggled and diminishing flow. With the final map, I call for the restoration of Hetch Hetchy Valley in Yosemite National Park as the most symbolically important restoration project on the table today. I close with a

of California's living systems

series of analysis models defending the general thesis of this book, that regardless of population growth and climate change, California has enough water to support the environment, the watersheds, wildlife, forests, and fisheries, as well as our agriculture and our cities. Whether we can support the historical model of unlimited growth is an entirely different matter.

For the past 170 years since the gold rush, California has never known anything but unlimited growth. That attitude is changing as we see an unraveling in the natural world. Because the network of life depends on natural systems and we are both responsible for and capable of mitigating their degradation, the case for maintaining, protecting, and even restoring as much biodiversity and habitat as we can is morally compelling and ethically imperative. Conservation science is revealing now how our human society is directly dependent on the subtle workings of a complex biosphere that relies on a myriad of networked connections to work correctly and to avoid collapse.

When it comes to our natural resources, we are in a time that demands of us advocacy for restoration over reclamation and for replenishment over extraction. I don't believe that arguing this is necessarily arguing against responsible and stable human industry and the managed use of these resources, including and most importantly water resources. Human society is built on the usage of these resources and will always be dependent on them, to varying degrees, for the functions they serve. To some measure, this book is an exercise in seeing how it plays out in terms of water and this search for a balanced give and take. This book holds a vision of the natural world in twenty-second-century California potentially being in better shape than it is in the twenty-first. In the next hundred years, as our society turns from extraction to replenishment as the primary attitude toward this giving land of plenty and moves into what will most probably morph into a post-carbon economy, we will reject more and more the rhetorical miasma set upon us as a divisive agenda from the swarm of professional politicians. The solutions to all manner of our ecological dilemmas are already on the table. Slowing the vocal extremes enough to listen to each other, we are one and we are not afraid of the work it will take to continue this, perhaps the most important conversation we can have.

California will rewild itself one way or another, eventually. Since the Miocene, over five million years ago, when California first began to resemble its current configuration, it began its process of island evolution. A long string of endemic speciation began its parade into existence west of the rising Sierra Nevada. Since then, cycles of ecological succession have been imposed like so many alarm clocks going off at regular intervals across millennia, dictating the climatic equilibrium of one age after the next. Things happen across California, but never to California. California forever abides until, several million years from now, it too will fade from cartographic recognition, swallowed into the larger tectonic system. We are another thing happening across California, akin to a flood or a fire. One day our tyranny of concrete and plastic will end and either we will be there with new systems of economy and governance, or we won't. My perspective is that California does not need to get right with us; it is wholly for us to learn to settle into these larger, living networks that will continue to afford us life and opportunity if we so choose.

The acre-foot

Except for when I am talking about per capita use, I don't measure water by liquid gallons or liters. This book measures water by acre-feet, or even more commonly, millions of acre-feet. An acre-foot of water equals about 326,000 gallons (1,234,044 liters), or enough water to cover an acre of land one foot (30.5 cm) deep. One acre-foot is used as a measure of strategy for stored water as the amount needed to meet the needs of one household of five people with a per capita usage at 178 gallons per day.[2] Since the scope of this book is to examine water systems across the state, I've standardized the use of the acronym MAF (million acre-feet), rounded to the nearest tenth decimal (for example, .01 MAF equals 10,000 acre-feet, and .14 MAF equals 140,000 acre-feet).

What is a watershed?

A watershed is a geographic area defined by how a single system of liquid water moves above and below ground to supply essential habitat for either a single ecosystem or a network of connected ecosystems. The word "shed" implies a container, an isolated and discreet investigable unit. Often described by topographic features, most often elevation increase by ridgeline, the boundaries of a watershed may also be drawn by soil types and aquifer size. A watershed can include many different climate types and run through many different environments yet is always connected by a common drainage. Watersheds can be examined at many different scales, from creeksheds measuring just a mile or two, to the Sacramento River Valley which encompasses 26,500 square miles.

PART ONE:
THE BIG PICTURE

Map 01.01

Water Yesterday, Water Today, Water Tomorrow

An overview of the state of water

The first water scenario in the book describes the geographic
context and proximity of the other eight. It includes three lake
systems that have been threatened (07. Mono Lake) or completely
decimated (16. Owens Lake and 17. Tulare Lake) by human
development, specifically the decision to urbanize the watersheds
of the Los Angeles and Santa Ana Rivers at the beginning of the
twentieth century, along with the agricultural development of the
western San Joaquin Valley. These three examples are included
in this map as they have all now reached a precarious plateau of
resolution, being emblematic of yesterday's (or tomorrow's) fights
for how we spend elements of the waterscape to whatever utilized
end, and either cast them into oblivion or preserve them as part of
California's natural legacy.

01. The Klamath River (see map 02.03). Beginning in 2020, the
Klamath will see the dismantling of four dams in its upper basin,
representing the largest salmonid habitat restoration project in
American history.[1] This after long negotiations and long controversy among tribes, environmental advocates, upriver irrigators,
and governments. Together with its major tributaries, including the

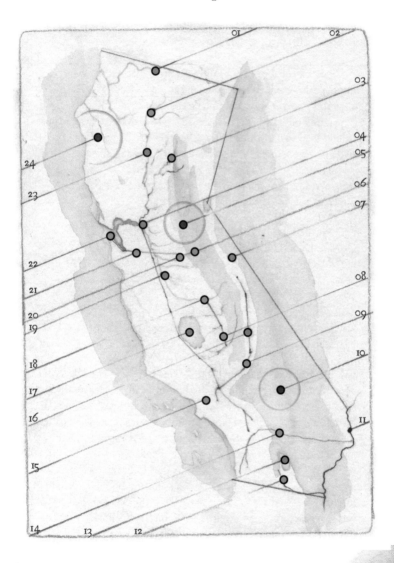

important, salmon-sustaining Trinity River, the Klamath River Basin is California's second largest watershed.

02. Shasta Dam (see map 02.01). California's largest reservoir, impounding water from the Sacramento, McCloud, and Pit Rivers. There is a proposal to increase the height of the dam, and depending on how high, to increase the capacity of the reservoir behind it to two or three times its current maximum. This expensive proposition is risky in that increasing the size of a reservoir doesn't create water—in fact it might result in a net water loss from evaporation—and it would destroy some of the best remaining trout habitat in California.[2]

03. Oroville Dam on the Feather River. Built fifty years ago, the Oroville Dam is the tallest in the United States at nearly 800 feet tall. The large spillway of this earthen dam threatened to fail after heavy rains in February 2017, and nearly 200,000 people were evacuated. We came close to realizing an unthinkable disaster. This crisis brings into sharp focus the need to assess an aging water infrastructure, especially with the emerging climate trend of increased episodes of aridity followed by larger moments of deluge.

04. The San Francisco Bay Delta (see map 02.02). The West's largest estuary, watered by the Sacramento and San Joaquin Rivers and their tributaries. In 1982 Californians voted down the first Peripheral Canal proposal, a plan to divert massive amounts of freshwater inflow from the delta to agricultural and urban interests in the south, threatening a potential collapse of the ecology within this vital estuary. This was the first California water project in history to not pass, a sign of shifting popular attitude toward water and the environment. The Peripheral Canal plan was most recently repackaged as California Water Fix and Eco Restore. The proposal includes construction of new large diversion

tunnels to take Sacramento River water south and is still being fought by tribes and most conservation groups as unacceptably damaging to this endangered habitat.[3]

05. The rivers of the Sierra, California's water tower. Thirteen rivers of the Sierra Nevada all flow roughly parallel to one another from east to west on their way to the Sacramento and San Joaquin Valleys to eventually find their outlet at the San Francisco Bay Delta. Together, these rivers are the source for more than 60% of California's developed water supply.[4]

06. Hetch Hetchy Reservoir (see map 04.01). Entirely within the borders of Yosemite National Park, Hetch Hetchy Reservoir, near the headwaters of the Tuolumne River, supplies 85% of the city of San Francisco's drinking water.[5] As upgrades to downstream reservoirs have come online, the people of California are changing their attitude about this reservoir's value and whether it still outweighs the value of restoration of the Hetch Hetchy Valley.

07. Mono Lake. A natural lake over one million years old that was, for most of the twentieth century, slowly disappearing due to the diversion of many of its tributary streams by the long straw of Los Angeles. Against all odds, a successful lawsuit brought against the thirsty city to the south by the Mono Lake Committee and the Audubon Society (who were in the fight to save the million migratory birds who nest and feed on the flies and shrimp in the lake) stopped the destruction of this ecological marvel. Since the court decision in 1994 that declared the lake is held in public trust and that it deserves to exist, restoration efforts have proceeded at a less than ideal pace, but for now have plateaued with a legally sound foothold.[6]

08. The Friant-Kern Canal (see map 02.02). One of the major arteries of water deliveries on the eastern slope of the San Joaquin Valley. With decades of back and forth legal decisions on how much water to release from Millerton Reservoir, delivery amounts on the canal have swung widely, leading to overdraft of already taxed groundwater supplies and subsidence of the canal itself.[7]

09. The Los Angeles Aqueduct (see map 01.03). The machine that made Los Angeles. Two aqueducts run from Owens Valley to Los Angeles. After diverting the Owens River in 1911, the first aqueduct drained Owens Lake (16), an ancient lake at the base of Mount Whitney, in just ten years. The second aqueduct was constructed in the 1950s. Together they currently deliver just about 35% of the city's water supply.[8]

10. The Mojave Desert. The largest physiographic region of California that remains entirely outside the boundaries of the California Floristic Province, but within California's political border. The two largest watersheds in this, California's most arid region, are the intermittent Mojave River and the Amargosa River near Death Valley, which exists on the border with Nevada's Great Basin Desert.

11. The Colorado River (see map 03.02). Outside of California, across the other six states that America's Nile flows through, the conversation about water in the West can begin and end with this mighty blue line.[9] Over the past hundred years, the average temperature in the Colorado River Basin has increased by 2°F and is expected to increase another 5°F by the end of the century; in that time frame, Colorado River flow will decrease between 10 and 20%.[10]

Striped bass
Morone saxatilis

12. The All-American Canal (see map 01.03). With less than three inches of annual rainfall, the Imperial Valley has used water from the Colorado River—delivered by the All-American Canal and its hundreds of miles of supplemental canals—to become one of the nation's primary agricultural regions.

13. The Salton Sea (see map 03.01). At the beginning of the twentieth century, a breach in a canal flooded the Salton Sink to form this immense pond. Now fed by agricultural runoff, the salinity of the lake is 25% higher than the ocean's.[11] A strange blight and yet an incredibly rich bird-wetland ecosystem, the Salton Sea shrinks now a bit every year, exposing its salty chemicals to wind and weather. Because of this, remediation of the highly influential Salton Sea should be one of the state's top ecological priorities.

14. The Colorado Aqueduct (see map 01.03). A key regional asset for the Metropolitan Water District (MWD) of Southern California.

North Fork, Yuba River, Summer 2018

Although Los Angeles plans to greatly increase and diversify the sources of its water over the next twenty years, for the 19 million users across MWD's six counties, this canal is currently vital. In Los Angeles, the current plan is for MWD deliveries to be reduced from 326KAF (1000 acre-feet) to 168KAF by 2034.[12]

15. City of Los Angeles. Population 2010: 9.84 million. Population projection 2060: 11.11 million (an increase of 11.4%) humans. In 2010, Los Angeles used 0.62 MAF of water—0.22 MAF (36%) came from the Owens Valley and the Los Angeles Aqueduct, 0.37 MAF (52%) came from the Feather River and the Colorado River, 0.07 MAF (11%) came from pumping local groundwater, and 0.01 MAF (1%) came from recycled water.[13]

16. Owens Lake and Valley (see map 01.03). Given the ample water, the good soil, and clockwork seasonality of this fertile valley, might it have become another agricultural powerhouse if Los Angeles didn't divert the Owens River in the early twentieth century? Now, a century later, some restoration and local control have returned to the valley in a precarious accord between further extraction and managed replenishment. The dry lakebed covering roughly 115,000 acres is one of the most polluted places for particulate dust in the country. Several thousand tons of fine, alkali grit annually blankets the adjacent landscape of the northern Mojave Desert.[14] Up the valley, the Lower Owens River Project is a 78,000-acre restoration project on the Owens River, and the fight continues to save the Blackrock Spring from perilous overdraft by an ever-growing Los Angeles. The city calls for more withdrawal from a current average of 221KAF to 244KAF in 2034.[15] Since Los Angeles owns the aqueduct, it is ultimately cheaper for the city than buying water through the Metropolitan Water District and the California State Water Project. A harrowing position for the recovering systems of the valley; perhaps even Mono Lake is not safe in this situation.

17. Tulare Lake. With the building of Pine Flat Dam on the Kings River in the forties, the end of Tulare Lake was at hand. Now we live with the ghost of California's largest lake under the cotton plantations of Kings County.[16] Flooding, the primary stated reason for the dam's construction, altered the hydrology of this endorheic basin for the foreseeable future. For millennia, Tulare Lake was the mouth for four of California's great rivers: the Kings, the Kaweah, the Tule, and the Kern. The western edge of the San Joaquin Valley, now an ostensible desert sustained only by managed water deliveries, was only one hundred years ago a sprawling wetland, home to thousands of tule elk and over 80 million migrating birds. Today it is arguably the hub of the most productive agricultural region in the world. The heart of the story of how Tulare Lake was given to this pervading idea of reclamation, of what we've given and what has been taken, is core to the discussion of where our society goes next.

18. Friant Dam (map 02.02). Before this keystone dam in the State Water Project was opened in 1949, half a million salmon a year headed up its length to their spawning ground. In the face of the extinction of San Joaquin Chinook salmon, we have relented, and we have compromised by letting some water go with the hope of restoring this ancient run. We are beginning to see important measures of life return to this watercourse, thanks to these restoration flows (which began in 2009), where water flows again for the first time in sixty years.[17] In 2017 we saw spring-run Chinook salmon spawn in the river for the first time since the dam's construction (albeit restarted with Feather River juvenile fish). This success comes at a huge monetary cost ($1.5 billion by 2025 when the project should be completed) and to the local agricultural industry who saw water deliveries drop in some cases 90% in ten years, mostly because of drought but in part to support this restoration effort.

19. The San Joaquin River (map 02.02). To look at maps of the winding and expansive wetlands that composed the San Joaquin Valley a hundred years ago, and to compare them now with the urban and irrigated landscape that stretches from east to west, up to the very edge of both sides of California's Great Central Valley, is to consider how completely, how uncompromisingly we've managed to harness the power of water. By any measure, the absolute reclamation of the valley and this strongest of the Sierra rivers is one of the most telling achievements of modern hydrology and engineering. Now, at the last hour as we watch the remnants of ancient ecosystems get lost to extinction, we are pulling back to wonder what we've lost and if there is any chance of at once saving a vestige of that legacy while maintaining the productivity we've achieved. All systems strive toward equilibrium. What is the productive equilibrium between industrial and ecological preservation is the most important question of the next hundred years.

20. Don Pedro Dam (see map 04.01). Holding the largest reservoir on the Tuolumne River, Don Pedro Dam is not part of the San Francisco water delivery system, as are the other five reservoirs upriver from it. A likely scenario in the restoration of Hetch Hetchy Valley is for the city of San Francisco to purchase 60,000 acre-feet of water from the Turlock Irrigation District, who owns Don Pedro, and build a tunnel from the reservoir to the Hetch Hetchy Aqueduct to deliver it and offset the deficit incurred by a restored Hetch Hetchy Valley.[18]

21. The Hetch Hetchy Aqueduct. Reservoirs in the Tuolumne watershed have a 2.70 MAF capacity and receive a mean annual flow of less than 2.00 MAF. Hetch Hetchy Reservoir provides 14% of reservoir storage in the watershed.[19]

Foresthill Bridge on the North Fork of the American River, at the confluence of the Middle Fork. The highest bridge in North America, built so high to accommodate the Auburn dam and its reservoir, that never happened—a symbol of what might have been lost and what has been saved.

22. City of San Francisco. Population 2010: .87 million. Population projection 2060: 1.17 million (an increase of 25%) humans. In 2015, San Francisco used 0.22 MAF of water, 85% of which was delivered from the Tuolumne watershed.[20]

23. The Sacramento River (see map 02.01). There are rivers in California, and then there is the Sacramento. With a natural average annual discharge of 22 MAF, the Sacramento River historically surges with a potency that rivals the Mississippi. Its longest tributary, the Pit River, begins its journey to the sea nearly 700 miles from the Sacramento's mouth in the San Francisco Bay Delta. Hundreds of miles of levees and dozens of dams and gates now hold the powerful Sacramento from extending across the valley to its historical maximum width of 30 miles during floods. Shasta Dam, at the northernmost point of the Sacramento Valley, is the largest reservoir in the State Water Project.

24. North Coast Rivers. The rivers that meet the ocean have fed the forests of the coast redwoods for millions of years. Described by some of our best writers as "without end"[21] or as if they represent a "knot"[22] of unprecedented, diverse life unfolded across tumbling wilderness, nine major rivers make it to the Pacific in the north state—among these are the Smith, Klamath, Mad, Eel, Mattole, and Russian. Nearly 40% of the state's total rain runoff falls in these often remote watersheds, home to the state's longest wild, undammed rivers, their tributaries, fisheries, wildlife, and human communities. One of the rivers belonging to the North Coast that does not reach the Pacific on its own but is an exemplar—for salmon, tribal rights, water law, the politics of diversions, and the health or ill-health of the Klamath Basin fishery—is the Trinity.

What is restoration?

Restoration is the practice of repairing a damaged or altered ecosystem to recreate a state of equilibrium between natural forces and mitigate negative impacts of human activity or other damage. Restoration enhances habitat for animal and plant species, expands wildlife corridors and habitat connectivity, and supports abiotic systems that species need to survive, including improved water quantity and quality, reestablishment of flooding and fire cycles, and remediation and prevention of pollution or toxins. Projects may include responses to botanical or biological invasions of nonnative species or pathogens, or cleanup, repair, and prevention of damage imposed by the human ecology such as an oil spill, deforestation of a watershed, damming a river, or obstructing migration.

Restoration projects in watersheds improve flows; restore channels and life-stage habitats; remove barriers to fish passage; remediate and control the effects of erosion and silt; remove nonnative plants and replant native species; and remove trash, waste, and toxic materials and prevent their introduction. Projects for forest health and protection of watersheds and their ecosystem benefits (such as reliability of water supplies, natural cycling of fresh water, carbon sequestration) promote climate and fire resilience via prescribed beneficial fire and forest fuels reduction, as well as protection of old-growth forest qualities, removal of roads and redesign of culverts, and strategies to manage forest diseases such as the nonnative pathogen causing Sudden Oak Death.[73]

Improving the quality and health of damaged habitat in our riparian areas and beyond is an increasing priority as we see the last pristine places struggle to maintain their original character and the in-between places suffer from our encroachment.

What is groundwater?

Groundwater is the portion of water (the majority of which is fresh) under the earth's surface held in the spaces and soils that compose the underground formations of sand, gravel, silt, and clay. These formations are called aquifers and can hold millions of acre-feet of water of several thousand cubic miles, and because of this nobody knows with really any degree of certainty how much water is underground. Hydrologists estimate that 30 percent of water in lakes and rivers comes from aquifers where the water table (the top of the aquifer) meets the surface. Although groundwater is recharged by snowmelt and rainwater, the rate at which it is being pumped and the amount of pavement covering recharge areas is so vast, groundwater use is mostly a one-time resource spend.[24] Because of lack of regulation and increased environmental flow allotments, it has been estimated that groundwater source usage has spiked to 64 percent of all water used in California.[25] Land subsidence due to groundwater overdraft has become a significant problem in the San Joaquin Valley.[26] With the passage of the Sustainable Groundwater Management Act in 2014, the California government seeks to, for the first time, sustainably regulate and monitor groundwater withdrawals and deposits.

Map 01.02

The Wild California Riverscape

The living circuit in the body of California

"It is hereby declared to be the policy of the United States that certain selected rivers of the Nation which, with their immediate environments, possess outstandingly remarkable scenic, recreational, geologic, fish and wildlife, historic, cultural or other similar values, shall be preserved in free-flowing condition, and that they and their immediate environments shall be protected for the benefit and enjoyment of present and future generations. The Congress declares that the established national policy of dams and other construction at appropriate sections of the rivers of the United States needs to be complemented by a policy that would preserve other selected rivers or sections thereof in their free-flowing condition to protect the water quality of such rivers and to fulfill other vital national conservation purposes." (Wild and Scenic Rivers Act, 1968)

Map 01.02 is a stylized rendering of the California riverscape where the watercourses themselves are enlarged enough to be visible at this scale. Rivers are treated with equal line weight without respect for the capacity of each river itself. How beautiful the virgin waterscape of California is! A circulatory system that feeds life to California's living body, despite all of our damming monuments, despite all of our mechanical diversions, despite all of our willful intentions to bend the natural world to our own will. In a thousand years, when our human influence on the landscape has evolved and transformed into the next phase of human ecology, we will be able to draw this map again and it will be remarkably identical.

Green Sturgeon
Acipenser medirostris

In accord with the agenda of this book, the cloistering, localized effect is the map's purpose: rivers occur mostly in the Sierra Nevada, the Northwest, and along the coast. The map's other purpose is to inventory and describe the locations of all twenty-three federally recognized wild and scenic rivers. There are no rivers in California that are designated wild and scenic from headwaters to mouth—instead, only segments are. California has approximately 189,454 miles of river, of which 1,999.6 miles are designated as wild and scenic—1 percent of the state's river miles.[1] Less than one quarter of 1 percent of the country's rivers are designated wild and scenic, so in this instance, California is ahead of the curve. The dramatic blue lines in this map belie how riparian ecosystems are critically endangered across California.

The designation of a wild and scenic river for riparian and riverine ecologies is not unlike the designation of wilderness areas across terrestrial ecologies. Both represent our highest ideals of stewardship, where we might just let nature be nature according to its own ancient ways. With the designation of wild and scenic comes a management classification: the total length of the designated stretch of river is divided between wild, scenic, and recreational. A wild river area is "free of impoundments and generally inaccessible except by trail, with watersheds or shorelines essentially primitive and waters unpolluted. These represent vestiges of primitive America." A scenic river area is defined similarly except "accessible in places by roads." A recreational river area is "readily accessible by road or railroad, that may have some development along its shorelines, and that may have undergone some impoundment or diversion in the past."[2] Although this important designation legally protects the waterway itself, logging, grazing, roadbuilding, and other human activities continue to significantly affect the watershed's ecology.

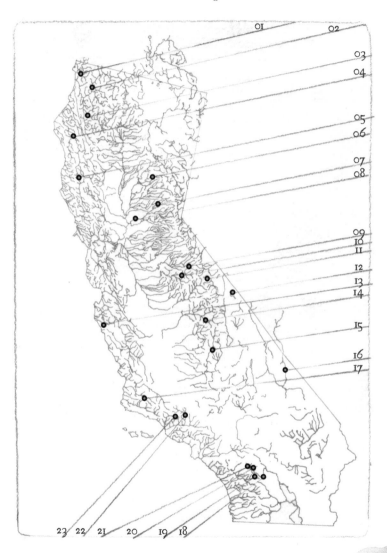

01. Smith River. Wild—78.0 miles; Scenic—31.0 miles; Recreational—216.4 miles; Total—325.4 miles.[3] The Smith is the largest river system in California that flows freely along its entire course.[4]

02. Klamath River. Wild—11.7 miles; Scenic—23.5 miles; Recreational—250.8; Total—286.0 miles. The Klamath's designated wild and scenic reach runs from below Iron Gate Dam (to be removed by 2020[5]) to its mouth on the coast and includes wild and scenic portions of the North and South Forks of the Salmon River, all of Wooley Creek, and portions of the Scott River.

03. Trinity River. Wild—44.0 miles; Scenic—39.0 miles; Recreational—120.0 miles; Total—203.0 miles. With increased environmental flows in the Trinity to protect this area's rich ecology and critical habitat for salmonid fisheries from toxic algae blooms and ever-increasing water temperatures, the Central Valley Project receives almost 4% less water per year since 2005.[6]

04. Eel River. Wild—97.0 miles; Scenic—28.0 miles; Recreational—273.0 miles; Total—398.0 miles. Old dams in the headwaters of this remote watershed send water to Mendocino and Sonoma counties. Larger dams were planned as part of the State Water Project but controversy led to federal wild and scenic protection. The Eel now enjoys more linear miles of this protection than any other river in California, yet suffers damage from logging and grazing as well as from water diversions, toxins, and siltation related to large-scale cannabis cultivation.[7]

05. Black Butte River. Wild—17.5 miles; Scenic—3.5 miles; Total—21.0 miles. A tributary of the lower fork of the Eel River, and a popular whitewater spot.

06. Feather River. Wild—32.9 miles; Scenic—9.7 miles; Recreational—35.0 miles; Total—77.6 miles. The entire length of the Middle Fork of the Feather River is wild and scenic.

07. American River (North Fork). Wild—38.3 miles; Total—38.3 miles. The full length of the North Fork of the American River is nearly 90 miles long. The reach that traces a deep line through one of the Sierra Nevada's most romantic canyons is the segment that is wild and scenic.

08. American River. Recreational—23.0 miles; Total—23.0 miles. From its confluence with the Sacramento River to Folsom Lake (the first obstacle to returning salmon), the American River is protected through its urban meanderings.

09. Tuolumne River. Wild—47.0 miles; Scenic—23.0 miles; Recreational—13.0 miles; Total—83.0 miles. The protected portion of the iconic river that provides water for San Francisco is designated in two divided parts: from its headwaters to Hetch Hetchy Reservoir in Yosemite National Park, and then again after the dam.

10. Merced River. Wild—71.0 miles; Scenic—16.0 miles; Recreational—35.5 miles; Total—122.5 miles. The Merced River made Yosemite Valley what it is with its slow cutting action through 200-million-year-old granite.

11. Owens River Headwaters. Wild—6.3 miles; Scenic—6.6 miles; Recreational—6.2 miles; Total—19.1 miles. From nearly 12,000 feet in elevation, the Owens River is protected as wild and scenic on the first leg of its trip toward diversion to Los Angeles through the aqueduct or into the fertile Owens Valley below.

12. Cottonwood Creek. Wild—17.4 miles; Recreational—4.1 miles; Total—21.5 miles. Cottonwood Creek feeds the bristlecone pines,

the oldest trees in the world, and provides habitat for one of the rarest fish in North America, the Paiute cutthroat trout.

13. Big Sur River. Wild—19.5 miles; Total—19.5 miles. Through the Ventana Wilderness, the two forks of this gem of coastal woodland habitat flow to where the wild and scenic designation ends at their confluence.

14. Kings River. Wild—65.5 miles; Recreational—15.5 miles; Total—81.0 miles. Through the second-deepest canyon in North America, the Kings River is protected for the entire length of its north and middle forks through Kings Canyon National Park.

15. Kern River. Wild—123.1 miles; Scenic—7.0 miles; Recreational—20.9 miles; Total—151.0 miles. Both forks of the Kern River include segments that are protected with a wild and scenic designation. Through the Golden Trout Wilderness, the North Fork may be the longest linear, glacially sculpted valley in the world. The South Fork runs through the Domeland Wilderness.

16. Amargosa River. Wild—7.9 miles; Scenic—12.1 miles; Recreational—6.3 miles; Total—26.3 miles. This treasure of desert riparian diversity has existed as a watershed for over eight thousand years. Endangered and threatened species who rely on this unique habitat include the Amargosa vole, the least Bell's vireo, the yellow-billed cuckoo, Swainson's hawk, Amargosa niterwort (a desert flower in the goosefoot family), the Amargosa pupfish, and the Amargosa speckled dace—the last two being small but tough fish.

17. Sisquoc River. Wild—33.0 miles; Total—33.0 miles. The condor-patrolled forests of the Los Padres National Forest hide

this perennial creek that has never known dam or diversion. The extant level of preservation on exhibit here is a wonderful tangle of black bears, brown trout, oaks, sycamores, and a vernal wildflower display that rivals anywhere in California's backcountry.

18. Palm Canyon Creek. Wild—8.1 miles; Total—8.1 miles. Near Palm Springs, Palm Canyon is home to the nation's largest fan palm oasis, two miles downstream on the Agua Caliente Indian Reservation, and provides critical habitat for the endangered peninsular bighorn sheep and a songbird called the southwestern willow flycatcher.

19. Bautista Creek. Recreational—9.8 miles; Total—9.8 miles. This stretch of riparian habitat harbors more endangered species than any other comparable area in the San Bernardino National Forest.

California gull
Larus californicus

20. Fuller Mill Creek. Scenic—2.6 miles; Recreational—0.9 miles; Total—3.5 miles. From San Jacinto Peak, this slice of wilderness is critical habitat—home to populations of many endangered species including the mountain yellow-legged frogs, the rubber boa, the San Bernardino flying squirrel, and "species of special concern" the California spotted owl.

21. San Jacinto River (North Fork). Wild—7.2 miles; Scenic—2.3 miles; Recreational—0.7 miles; Total—10.2 miles. Meets the wild and scenic Fuller Mill Creek at the confluence of these two rivers for an essential wildlife corridor.

22. Piru Creek. Wild—4.3 miles; Recreational—3.0 miles; Total—7.3 miles. Downstream from Pyramid Lake, this creek is managed for wild trout for anglers and runs on the border between Los Angeles and Ventura counties.

23. Sespe Creek. Wild—27.5 miles; Scenic—4.0 miles; Total—31.5 miles. Sespe Creek is one of the only spawning grounds for the endangered southern steelhead trout, which migrates from the Pacific Ocean up the Santa Clara River and into Sespe Creek to spawn. The creek also supports one of the largest populations of endangered arroyo toads within a hundred-mile radius.

California least tern
Sterula antillarum browni

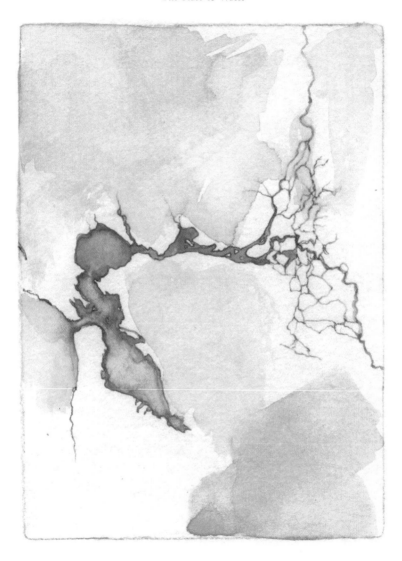

The Delta

With over four million people currently living in a highly urbanized community surrounding all corners of the San Francisco Bay Delta, it is a wonder that this sensitive estuary—home to so many threatened creatures including otters, smelt, and salmon—has not already succumbed to an ecological disaster of a more terrifying scope. The modicum of freshwater inflow that San Francisco Bay receives, as the mouth for both the Sacramento River and the San Joaquin River, is not enough to keep the salinity value of this system to historic, optimized levels. The bay itself, as a living estuary, is just about as old as the human communities that began living here about ten thousand years ago at the end of the Ice Age, when sea levels established present-day conditions. The Ohlone people, as they still call themselves, created large, populous, and vibrant communities for thousands of years on the shores of this incredibly productive foodshed. The delta is a place of nutrients, where the rivers bring life to the edge of the continent and create a unique habitat on a scale that no other river system can match on the western coasts of North and South America.

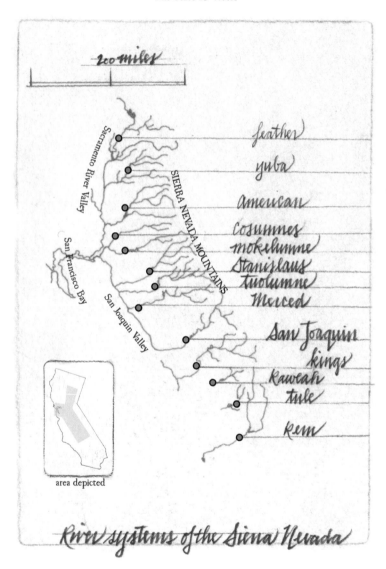

200 miles

Sacramento River Valley

San Francisco Bay

San Joaquin Valley

SIERRA NEVADA MOUNTAINS

feather

yuba

american

cosumnes
mokelumne
Stanislaus
tuolumne
Merced

San Joaquin

kings

Kaweah

tule

Kern

area depicted

River systems of the Sierra Nevada

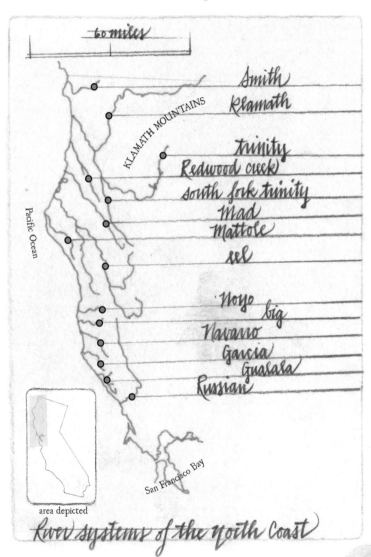

river systems of the north Coast

Shasta Dam obj Kaufmann 2018

Map 01.03
California's Water Projects

The geography of the California water machine

This is the machine, the engineered system of water conveyance that made California what it is today: a state as unsurpassed in its achievements of economy and civilization as its natural world is superlative in its diversity and grandeur.[1] In the last half of the twentieth century, water's negotiated allotment statewide was worked out, and when it wasn't, our hydrologic resources were split again and again until the whole system looked like an infinitely monopolized system of fractionated capillaries.

The system is so encompassing that it can be demonstrably argued that every drop of rainfall is not only managed but sold and resold, while allocations exceed available water resources.[2] Now that the climate is changing,[3] as are our values,[4] we realize that our rigid infrastructure is at once not as resilient or as accommodating as it needs to be to serve the coequal goals of withstanding the mounting, immediate pressure of increased drought, population growth, and biodiversity conservation.[5] We are seeing that the idea of a rigid infrastructure as the only defense to our precarious water is not a good bet.[6]

California has about 42 MAF of storage capacity in its reservoirs to defend against drought.[7] We keep approximately 16 MAF in surface reservoirs to carry over from wet to dry years for droughts lasting three to six years. These storage numbers don't include aquifer (groundwater) storage.

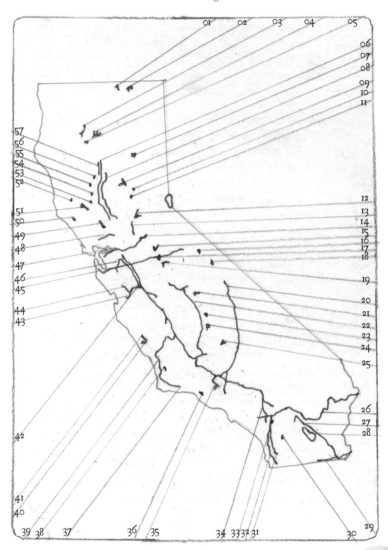

(s) – (size): reservoir capacity in million acre-feet (MAF). Typical indoor use per person ranges from 60 gallons/day to 200 gallons/day.[8] Irrigation toward fire-safe landscaping accounts for nearly half of residential water use. A good way to think of it is a single person uses one quarter of one acre-foot per year.

(h) – (hydroelectric): power-generating capacity in megawatts (MW). With 287 hydroelectric plants, California can potentially generate 21,000 MW, but regularly generates closer to 14,000 MW, or 6% of the total in-state electricity generation. California is working toward an energy mandate to source half of its electricity from clean renewable sources by 2030.[9] Big dams are out. Small hydro is in (operations 30 MW or smaller) for a total of 1,300 MW.[10] Reservoirs behind hydroelectric dams expel large amounts of methane gas, a key climate-change contributor.[11] To make matters worse, toxic algae from reservoirs is a problem for wildlife habitat and our health, and bacteria present in decaying vegetation can make mercury in the bedrock under a reservoir water-soluble.[12]

(p) – purpose: the reasons behind construction and continued operation. Individual projects can have multiple purposes and managers. The more purposes a given project has, the less likely it is to become obsolete.

a. CVP – the Central Valley Project, a federal water management system. Capture and storage for agricultural irrigation delivered to the Central Valley.

b. CSWP – California State Water Project. Capture and storage for municipal water and agricultural irrigation, half of which is delivered to Los Angeles—the Southern California Metropolitan Water District is allocated just around 2.00 MAF from this project per year.[13] The total delivering capacity of the project is 4.20 MAF.[14]

c. FWP – Federal Water Project. The federal government helped pay for construction or currently helps to manage, or both.

d. LWP – Local Water Project. Drinking water or local irrigation.

e. Flood control

f. Recreation

g. Groundwater recharge

h. Wildlife conservation

Note: There is a big difference between a lake and a reservoir. Discounting glacial headwater lakes in the Sierra, only Clear Lake in Lake County is part of any water delivery system. Natural lakes are vibrant and ancient parts of the local watershed. Reservoirs exist behind dams and cut the living artery of the river. In the list below, the word "lake" is replaced with the word "reservoir" unless it appears in proper names, as in Lake Almanor or Lake Casitas.

01. Tule Lake. Tule Lake National Wildlife Refuge: (s) 39,116 acres; (p) FWP, wildlife conservation, irrigation for 17,000 local farming acres.

02. Clear Lake Reservoir and Dam. River: the Lost River, (s) 0.52 MAF; (p) FWP, irrigation for the eastern half of the Klamath Basin.

03. Trinity Reservoir and Dam. River: Trinity, (s) 2.45 MAF; (p) CVP, FWP for irrigation in Central/Southern California; recreation; (h) 140 MW.

04. Shasta Reservoir and Dam. Rivers: Pit, Sacramento, McCloud, (s) 4.55 MAF; (p) CVP, FWP, 41% of the stored water of the CVP; for irrigation in Central/Southern California; hydroelectric; recreation, flood control; (h) 379 MW.

05. Whiskeytown Reservoir and Dam, Whiskeytown National Recreation Area. Rivers: Trinity, Clear Creek. Water is sourced from the diverted Trinity River through the Clear Creek Tunnel under Lewiston Lake, (s) 2.41 MAF; (p) CVP, FWP for irrigation in Central/Southern California; recreation, flood control; (h) 154 MW.

06. Tehama-Colusa Canal. Length: 140 miles; service area: 150,000 acres. Site of the Red Bluff Diversion Dam (RBDD) Fish Passage Improvement Project (see map 02.01); adjacent to Sites Dam Project*; (p) CVP, FWP.

07. Lake Almanor and Canyon Dam/Butt Valley Powerhouse. River: North Fork of the Feather, (s) 1.31 MAF; (p) LWP, recreation; (h) 41 MW.

08. Glenn-Colusa Canal. Length: 65 miles; service area: 175,000 acres; adjacent to Sites Dam Project*; (p) LWP.

09. Lake Oroville and Dam. River: Feather, (s) 3.50 MAF; (p) CSWP, CVP, recreation; (h) 519 MW.

10. New Bullards Bar Reservoir. River: North Yuba, (s) 0.97 MAF; (p) LWP, municipal; (h) 340 MW.

11. Englebright Reservoir. River: Yuba, (s) 0.07 MAF; (p) FWP, recreation; (h) 15 MW.

12. Folsom Reservoir and Dam. River: American, (s) 0.98 MAF; (p) CVP, FWP, flood control, recreation, municipal; (h) 199 MW.

13. Folsom South Canal. Length: 27 miles; service area: 7,000 acres; (p) CVP, FWP.

14. Comanche Reservoir and Dam. River: Mokelumne, (s) 0.47 MAF; (p) LWP, municipal drinking water for the East Bay Municipal Utility District, recreation.

15. New Melones Reservoir and Dam. River: Stanislaus, (s) 2.40 MAF; (p) CVP, FWP, recreation; (h) 300 MW.

16. Grant Lake, 1,100-acre recreational lake built on Rush Creek in 1916; (p) LWP.

17. New Don Pedro Reservoir (Hetch Hetchy Aqueduct). River: Tuolumne, (s) 2.03 MAF; (p) LWP, municipal; (h) 203 MW.

18. Crowley Reservoir and Long Valley Dam. River: upper Owens; part of the Los Angeles Aqueduct, (s) .18 MAF; (p) LWP, municipal, recreation.

19. Lake McClure and New Exchequer Dam. River: Merced, (s) 1.03 MAF; (p) LWP, municipal; (h) 95 MW.

20. Los Angeles Aqueduct: Owens Valley Aqueduct, 1913. Length: 233 miles long. Responsible for the devastation of the Owens Lake ecosystem; second Los Angeles Aqueduct, 1956; (p) LWP.

21. Pine Flat Reservoir and Dam. River: Kings, (s) 1.00 MAF; (p) FWP, flood control, groundwater recharge, recreation; (h) 165 MW.

22. Friant-Kern Canal: from Millerton Lake to Bakersfield, the canal is a major conduit of agricultural water across the eastern San Joaquin Valley. Length: 152 miles, (p) CVP, FWP; deliveries in 2005 were 1.72 MAF; deliveries in in 2015 were 0.06 MAF.

23. Kaweah Reservoir and Terminus Dam. River: Kaweah, (s) 0.19 MAF; (p) FWP, flood protection.

24. Success Reservoir and Dam. River: Tule, (s) 0.08 MAF; (p) FWP, LWP, flood protection.

25. Isabella Reservoir** and Dam. River: Kern, (s) 0.57 MAF; (p) FWP, LWP for Bakersfield, recreation.

26. Colorado River Aqueduct. Length: 242 miles. Begins at Lake Havasu (see map 04.02) to Lake Matthews. (p) LWP for Los Angeles (Metropolitan Water District of Southern California (MWD) and San Diego. Average annual delivery 1.20 MAF.

27. Coachella Canal. Length: 122 miles, (p) FWP, LWP for Coachella Valley from the Colorado River (Imperial Dam); annual deliveries average 0.29 MAF.

28. Salton Sea (see map 03.01).

29. All-American Canal. Length: 80 miles; (p) FWP, LWP for Imperial Valley from the Colorado River (Imperial Dam); (h) 58 MW; annual deliveries average 3.10 MAF.

30. Henshaw Reservoir** and Dam. Groundwater dam, (s) 0.06 MAF; (p) LWP, groundwater storage, recreation.
31. San Vincente Reservoir and Dam. River: San Vicente Creek, (s) 0.25 MAF; (p) LWP, recreation.

32. San Diego Aqueducts (Lower Otay Reservoir). Four aqueducts from the Colorado River that supply 90% of San Diego's water. Lower Otay Reservoir and Savage Dam. River: Otay River, (s) 0.05 MAF.

33. Diamond Valley Reservoir and West Dam, East Dam, Saddle Dam. Three dams for this off-stream reservoir filled by the Colorado Aqueduct, (s) 0.80 MAF; (p) LWP, recreation; (h) 40 MW.

34. California Aqueduct. The 400-mile main conduit of the California State Water Project. Begins at Clifton Court Forebay in the Sacramento–San Joaquin River Delta. The longest branch ends at Lake Perris**; (s) 0.13 MAF. Operated by the California Department of Water Resources (DWR).

35. Pyramid Reservoir and Dam. River: Piru Creek, (s) 0.18 MAF; (p) CSWP, recreation. On the West Branch of the California Aqueduct, (h) 1247 MW; Castaic Reservoir and Dam. River: Castaic Creek, (s) 0.32 MAF; (p), CSWP, recreation.

36. Lake Casitas and Dam. River: Coyote Creek, (s) 0.25 MAF; (p) FWP, LWP, flood control.

37. Cachuma Reservoir** and Bradbury Dam. River: Santa Ynez, (s) 0.21 MAF; (p) FWP, LWP, recreation.

38. Twitchell Reservoir** and Dam. River: Cuyama, (s) 0.23 MAF; (p) FWP, flood control, groundwater recharge.

39. Coastal Branch Aqueduct. Length: 116 miles from southeast of Kettleman City to its terminus at Vandenberg Air Force Base in Santa Barbara County, (p) CSWP, LWP for Kern, Santa Barbara, and San Luis Obispo counties.

40. Nacimiento Reservoir and Dam. River: Nacimiento, Snake Creek, Dip Creek, Las Tablas Creek, Franklin Creek, (s) 0.38 MAF; (p) LWP, recreation (although fish levels remain low due to mercury levels in the lake from local, now closed, mining).

41. San Antonio Reservoir and Dam. River: San Antonio, (s) 0.35 MAF; (p) LWP, groundwater recharge, recreation (although the reservoir is regularly closed due to low water levels).

42. San Luis Reservoir and Dam. Largest off-stream reservoir in the United States, (s) 2.04 MAF; CVP, CSWP, FWP; central hub of the water system; (h) 424 MW.

43. Hollister Conduit, (p) CVP, off-stream water storage; San Justo Reservoir closed due to zebra mussel infestation.

44. Santa Clara Conduit and tunnel, (p) CSWP, FWP, LWP pumps water to Santa Clara Valley.

45. Delta-Mendota Canal. Length: 117 miles from Tracy to the Mendota Pool (see map 02.02), (p) CVP, FWP, to replace water in the San Joaquin otherwise stopped because of Friant Dam and its canals.

46. South Bay Aqueduct. Length: 40 miles, (p) CSWP, to deliver water from local reservoirs to Alameda and Santa Clara counties.

47. Mokelumne Aqueduct (Contra Costa Canal). Length: 95 miles,

(p) LWP, delivers 0.36 MAF to 1.5 million people in the East Bay from the Mokelumne River and potentially, in dry years, the American River.

48. North Bay Aqueduct. Length: 28 miles, (p) CSWP, LWP, serves Napa and Solano counties.

49. Lake Berryessa and Monticello Dam. River: Putah Creek, Pope Creek, Capell Creek, and Eticuera Creek, (s) 1.60 MAF; FWP, LWP, flood control, groundwater recharge, recreation; (h) 12 MW.

50. Lake Sonoma and Warm Springs Dam, (s) 0.38 MAF; (p) FPW, LWP, recreation flood control; (h) 2.6 MW.

51. Clear Lake (Lake County). Natural lake; outflow through dam to maintain lake level, (p) flood control, recreation.

52. Lake Mendocino and Coyote Valley Dam, (s) .012 MAF; (p) flood control, recreation; (h) 2.6 MW.

53. Indian Valley Reservoir and Dam. River: Cache Creek, (s) 0.30 MAF; LWP for Yolo County, recreation.

54. East Park Reservoir and Dam. River: Indian Creek, (s) .05 MAF; FWP, LWP, recreation.

55. Stoney Gorge Reservoir. River: Salt Creek, (s) .06 MAF; FWP, LWP, recreation.

56. Black Butte Reservoir. River: Stony Creek, (s) 0.14 MAF; FWP, flood protection.

57. Corning Canal, (p) FWP, CVP, irrigation diversion from the Red Bluff Diversion Dam (see map 02.01).

(*) Sites Dam Project (proposed). River: off-stream reservoir; would impact flows in Sacramento River and other northern rivers; (s) between 1.27 and 1.81 MAF. This project, along with the California Water Fix (see map 02.02), is part of a larger plan to export Northern California water to offset declining allocations from the Colorado to agribusiness. This project will negatively affect the habitat of twenty-three sensitive, threatened, or endangered species.[15]

(**) Seismic concerns or sediment accumulation have compromised the integrity and capacity of these aging projects, which now realize only a partial amount of total potential storage.[16]

Chinook Salmon
Oncorhynchus tshawytscha

Chinook Salmon

In the salmon dream, if there is a bright, swirling center of the universe, this is it. The gravity of all the snow in the Sierra Nevada coming to meet its prismatic, brackish next phase is luminous under the gate. I trust this. I trust this place. The plan from Sacramento to further twist the water from its already overtaxed rivers, thirsty for their freer, former selves is hidden in words like "fix" and "eco" and comes falsely with looming pretense. Water, always the commodity, rarely the honored vehicle of all life. If genuine restoration is the goal, the solutions of conservation and efficiency are at hand, reflected in our hearts that sing, have sung, and will always sing trust in this place.

PART TWO:
THE NORTHERN RIVERS

Map 02.01

Salmon and the Sacramento

A measure of health in California's natural world

No creature better symbolizes the state of water ecology in
California, its struggle, and its decline than the California salmon.
Fourteen different populations of over three different species
have called this place home for millions of years.[1] Where only one
hundred years ago the Sacramento, the San Joaquin, the Klamath,
and other California rivers were run by millions of these fascinat-
ing fish, now wild populations dwindle unsustainably, numbering
in the thousands or less.[2] California salmon face challenges at every
developmental stage of their complex life cycle, from eggs, fry,
smolts, ocean subadults, to mature adults; and across all geographic states of their habitat including tributary streams, cold
water refugia at stream mouths, mainstem river, floodplain, delta,
bays, and ocean. Salmon require at every life stage and across
every habitat specific conditions of water velocity, depth, salinity,
and have specific temperature preferences and tolerances.[3] Habitat
impediments (dams), habitat degradation, habitat loss, commercial
and recreational fishing, and climate change are among the many
challenges that these species face, all of which humanity has power
to determine.[4]

Conservation biology is the science of saving endangered species and the biotic relationships that sustain those species. The science is based, in part, on humans providing functions that the natural world can either no longer provide or will not be able to provide in the foreseeable future. This has led to the setting up of new fishery strategies based on augmenting natural populations. Although five major fish hatcheries in the Sacramento Valley grow and release millions of smolts (baby salmon) each year, only a tiny fraction of 1 percent of any of these salmon return, and if they do, they are unable to get to the cold and clear upstream water they need to spawn.[5]

Across the Sacramento River watershed, heroic efforts are being made to create the facsimile of salmon spawning habitat, either by construction or restoration—like inviting them back to their newly remodeled home. We're working to save the two dozen genetically distinct populations of salmon we have in California that have lived in these rivers for the past six million years. The connection we feel to salmon runs deep and the decimation of the Pacific salmon population in California is deeply tragic. Ten evolutionarily significant units of salmon populations are now listed as either threatened or endangered by the state of California or by the federal government.[6] What will we have lost if the wild runs finally go extinct? Imagine the security offered by restored and thriving populations of anadromous fish—what that would mean for our roles as good stewards to this system—what that means for the health of the environment (clean water, food security, biodiversity, a sustainable future economy) and our incorporated role. Salmon are both indicator and keystone species. Their role as an indicator species is measured by their need for cold and clear water to reproduce. Their vitality is the best measure of environmental health throughout the riverine ecosystem. Their role as a keystone species is measured by how their numbers support diets

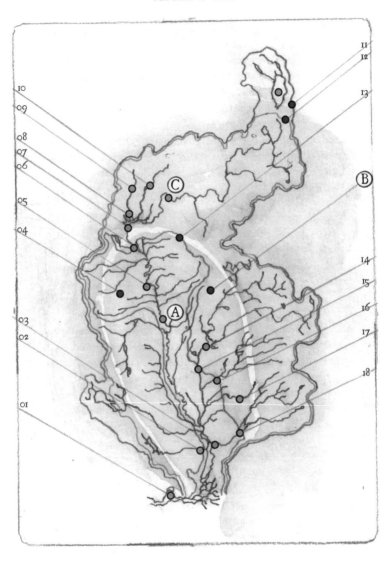

for entire populations of mammals and birds. The nitrogen their bodies give after they spawn is a vital nutrient for riparian forests, moved upslope by bears, ravens, and other creatures. Without salmon, the ecosystem collapses. When dominoes begin to fall and ecosystems begin to collapse, who is to say how it might end? Saving the salmon is as much about saving ourselves as it is anything else.

A. Sacramento River

B. Sacramento River Valley

C. Pit River

01. Suisun Marsh. Young salmon require the nutrients afforded by the San Francisco Bay estuary on their way out to sea from their hatching ground. Restoration efforts at Prospect Island near the Yolo Bypass are underway to augment this important habitat.[7]

02. Putah Diversion Dam. The first significant obstacle to returning salmon's passage northward from the bay; creates Lake Sonoma, a recreational lake.

03. Sacramento. The urban capital of California in the Sacramento floodplain that only survives because of flood-control dams and a labyrinth of levees.

04. Sunflower Coordinated Resource Management Program. A new kind of conservation group, state supported, managed by landowners. A coordinated resources program with an ambitious agenda toward the conservation of water and wildlife resources.[8]

05. Red Bluff Diversion Dam. One of the most damaging projects

to salmon populations before it was closed in 2011 and the gates were opened permanently to welcome returning salmon.

06. Redding.

07. Shasta Dam (see map 01.01) and the Iron Mountain Mine Superfund Cleanup.[9] Toxic damage from the zinc and copper mine, which operated for seventy years over the first half of the twentieth century, has led to an ongoing remediation effort.

08. Lake Shasta. California's largest reservoir. Even with environmental release flows of water for salmon, the temperature is often too warm for salmon spawning and smolt (young salmon) survival.[10]

09. The Sacramento River. Before 1850, in its biggest flood years the river would regularly fill its floodplain, 30 miles across. Restoring some remnants of the floodplain may be key to returning the salmon to viable, wild populations.[11]

10. McCloud River. Historically a spawning watershed for millions of salmon.

11. Sacramento River watershed. Habitat for 50% of the threatened and endangered species in California.

12. Historic range of the fall-, winter-, and spring-run Chinook salmon ESU (evolutionarily significant unit). Over the last forty years estimates of winter-run salmon on the Sacramento River have dropped over 90%.[12]

13. Current range of the fall-, winter-, and spring-run Chinook salmon ESU.

14. Feather River Hatchery. State and federal hatcheries will be responsible this year for the release of 40 million juvenile fall-run Chinook salmon into California waters.[13]

15. Feather River. The main tributary to the Sacramento River. The Feather's flows are much reduced by agricultural diversion south for the California State Water Project.

16. Englebright Dam. This reservoir is nearly half-full of sediment.

17. Centennial Dam (site). A questionable water project proposal.

18. Nimbus Dam. The first dam that returning salmon encounter on the American River, preventing them from progressing upstream.

Northern shoveler
anas clypeata

Coho Salmon
Oncorhynchus kisutch

Smelt

I am a child of the West, specifically California. I was born in 1973, the same year as the passage of the Endangered Species Act, in a brief time in the early 1970s called by some "the Golden Age of Environmental Legislation." Since then, in my country, I've watch the slow estrangement of half of our government turning from any policy deemed environmental. The whole dysfunctional system resembles a family squabble and the entrenched vocabulary we use to describe the political dynamic exacerbates the situation, infecting it to such a degree that often arguments, rooted in punditry, become an ineffectual din.

The language of this cultural polarization, which has trickled down from our government particularly with respect to all things having to do with the environment, is rooted in capitalist salesmanship. The relativism of the moral context, where all evil is defined by what may undermine any special interest, is exploited by professional politicians to the detriment of the common good. The core idea that the health, robustness, and resiliency of the natural world inexorably means the same for the human world is so basic an idea that to argue it politically is to expose a system so laden with an obsession for fractionating profit that its heart must be rotten and deserves to be cut out. We begin with the words and the art—remember, they are all we've got. Two words need to be remade: both environmentalism and sustainability have been appropriated by the antagonists of what the words signify. The (environmental and the coming post-environmental) movement itself needs to abandon them. They now are employed as dog-whistle words for propaganda against the movement to designate a whole set of dogmatic baggage unrelated to the movement itself. To again approach the moral imperative of how to best steer the ship away from the tyranny of its extraction-over-replenishment vector, we (all of us) need to uncouple the movement from any other order of the day.

Long Fin Smelt
Spirinchus thaleichthys

Delta Smelt
Hypomesus transpacificus

Map 02.02

Restoration of the San Joaquin

Mapping decisions of the valley's past and future legacy

There is no part of California as unrecognizable from the way it looked and functioned one hundred years ago than the San Joaquin Valley. Where once was a labyrinthine network of tule reed–covered wetlands, millions of acres of migratory bird habitat, and hundreds of miles of riverine habitat that supported runs of salmon that numbered in the millions, now neatly arranged farms take advantage of fecund soil and a regular Mediterranean climate to produce a disproportionate amount of the national food supply.

The single reason for this massive transformation is water diversion. After a century of reclamation, the process by which humans have manipulated natural water courses for agricultural and municipal needs, the San Joaquin River has been so altered that it is not even its own water that flows down much of its length. After being diverted by Friant Dam (no. 07 on map 02.02), the river doesn't exist for sixty miles (although since 2009, the dam began releasing water in ever-increasing quantities, to a current maximum of almost .30 MAF/year).[1] Then at the Mendota Pool (10), it begins to flow again with water from the Sacramento River pumped via the 117-mile-long Delta-Mendota Canal (12).[2]

When we consider what irreplaceable pieces of California's natural legacy we might be losing, it can be said that our moral conscience spurs us to turn from reclamation to restoration. If that is the case, what does restoration look like in landscapes that are so forever altered, so unrecognizable that there doesn't seem to be any original character left to restore? We've placed a lot of weight on the

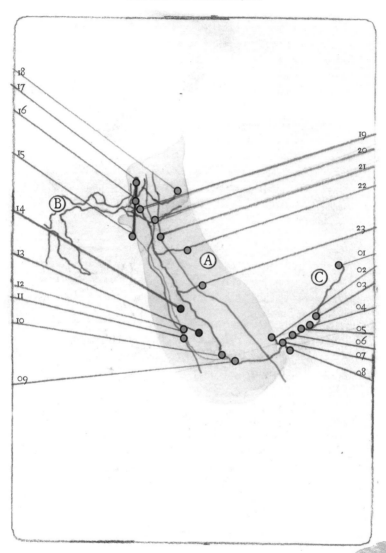

charismatic salmon to be the symbol of this yearning to hold onto what might otherwise be lost forever, and there is a light of hope. In December of 2017, for the first time in sixty years, spring-run Chinook salmon spawned in the San Joaquin River.[3] The massive human effort involved introducing juvenile salmon from the Feather River Hatchery in preceding years and later transporting, by truck, the adult salmon who were able to return up the river to spawn because a good rain year reconnected it with the sea. The trucked salmon were moved around the many obstacles—dams and diversions—and released just below Friant Dam, which is now releasing measured amounts of water, called restoration flows, for this endeavor. Once released, the salmon spawned and completed their life cycle.

What it amounts to is a point proven, if albeit novel and tenuous: we can work to simultaneously invent and restore a new biodiverse vision of the San Joaquin River Valley. This new vision can sustain industry and abundant habitat for hundreds of future generations, both fish and human.

A. San Joaquin Valley. Despite the perception that the history of farming in California is a history of monopolism and massive, corporate agribusiness, upward of 90% of farms in the valley are family owned.[4]

B. San Francisco Bay. Habitat for the delta smelt, a tiny endangered fish that is protected by federal law. Protecting the delta smelt is about more than protecting the one species—the spirit of the Endangered Species Act assures that the protection of habitat is a coequal goal.[5] Protecting the smelt means protecting clean water that filters pollution in healthy bay tidal marshes and curbs global warming by storing carbon in these same marshes; providing habitat for hundreds of other species, protecting human

american avocet
Recurvirostra americana

communities from floods and sea level rise by ensuring robust marshland ecosystems; providing the legacy of the intrinsic and invaluable natural landscape; and protecting the local industries of tourism, fishing, and recreation.

C. The Sierra Nevada. What gives California its arid or fertile, isolated character is written across the natural topography of the land itself. Our state enjoys a nature-built water tower in the form of the continent's longest contiguous mountain range, the Sierra Nevada.

01. Thousand Island Lake, headwaters of the San Joaquin River in the John Muir Wilderness.

02. Madera Canal, 40-mile irrigation conveyance northward out of Friant Dam.

03. Mammoth Pool Reservoir and Dam; (s) 0.12 MAF; (p) recreation; (h) 190 MW.

04. Redinger Reservoir and Dam. Above Millerton Reservoir, Southern California Edison built the Big Creek Hydroelectric Project, twenty-seven dams that produce more than 10% of California's hydroelectric power.

05. Kerckhoff Reservoir, another piece of the Big Creek Hydroelectric Project.

06. Temperance Flat (proposed site). If built, this fiasco of a project would cost billions, never fill, impact the deliverable energy from the upstream hydroelectric, and destroy eight miles of riparian forest along the river.[6]

07. Friant Dam. When we built Friant Dam, we explicitly understood that we were condemning salmon in the San Joaquin River.[7] This extractive mindset that pays no mind to replenishment or conservation, that says the workings of the natural world are for our own one-time use, is an anachronism of unwise, greedy, and ultimately dangerous thinking. In this case, a lawsuit led to the interagency project to restore salmon to the San Joaquin.

08. The Friant-Kern Canal. Takes nearly all the San Joaquin River from behind Friant Dam, leaving the river dry for nearly 60 miles past the reservoir.

09. Gravelly Ford, where the river dries up in the summer.

10. Mendota Pool, where imported water flows into the river channel.

11. Interstate 5, where billboards claim that Congress is creating a dustbowl and that water equals jobs and that more water storage is the answer.[8]

12. Delta-Mendota Canal

13. Los Banos Waterfowl Management Area, 6,000 acres along the Pacific Flyway. Home to several hundred species of birds and wildlife.

14. San Luis National Wildlife Refuge, 30,000 acres of protected habitat.

15. Clifton Court Forebay. Intake reservoir for the California Aqueduct and the Delta-Mendota recharge canal.

16. California Water Fix and Eco Restore, proposed site. A massively expensive project that doesn't fix California's water woes and does little in the way of ecological restoration to countermeasure the damage this project would inflict. Compromises to the delicate balance between fresh and salt water in the San Francisco Bay Delta potentially put this ecosystem on the brink of collapse. The solution proposed by the state government is called the Water Fix and Eco Restore.[9] This is a new version of a forty-year-old idea.[10] The plan calls for underground conveyance—tunnels—to deliver water from the Sacramento into the State Water Project.[11] The plan is that with the tunnels in place, the ecological devastation of the Jones Pumping Plant[12] at the Delta-Mendota Canal (12) can be mitigated and tidal flows can be restored in the south delta, 30,000 acres of wetland (14) can be restored and protected,[13] and there will be less pressure on the aging infrastructure of levees across the region.[14] The not-so-secret, other purpose of WaterFix is the water security of Los Angeles into the future.[15] The problem is that if too much water is taken—nobody really knows how much that is—the effects could be devastating. It is a terribly expensive gamble. If the eco-health of the delta is the primary concern, a simpler plan would involve investing in levee reinforcement, increasing natural flows of fresh water, increasing reliance on local water supply, and improving water capture, storage, and conservation.[16]

17. Tunnel intakes (proposed site).

18. Mokelumne River.

19. The entrance of the San Francisco Bay Delta.

20. Cosumnes River.

American Widgeon
Anas americana

American Shad
Alosa sapidissima

Tule elk
Cervus canadensis nannodes

Tule Elk

*My study has always been love. Press me and
I begin to murmur things like how my work
is not science, but the subject of my work is
data-driven biodiversity. I study patterns of
habitat. To be more specific, I am a student of
the beauty and history of biological evolution in
morphological architecture and its application
to fitness strategy across living systems. In
my art and writing about ecology, I am more
satisfied with the exploration of the best, most
simple and elegant question than I am with any
righteous, vocational answer.*

Map 02.03

Emancipation of the Klamath

The largest dam removal in American history

It isn't about one species; the restoration of the Klamath River
ecosystem is about good stewardship.[1] Species such as the salmonids, by their presence alone, grade us on this stewardship. Without them, we will have lost one of the key markers of the quality
of the local, ecological vitality and its continuing fecundity. Of
all the challenges these ancient, diverse species of Chinook, coho,
and steelhead endure, including habitat loss and inaccessibility
from dams and development, warmer water temperatures from
dams, diversions, and global warming, predation of juvenile fish
by invasive species, crude designs of ineffectual assistance such
as insufficient fish ladders, watercourse pollution and poisoning
from agricultural and urban runoff[2]—and of course the big one,
drought—the single biggest threat they face is the human attitude
toward the problem.[3] This threat is also the one that in theory is
the most easily removed.

01. Klamath River. North of the Sacramento River, the Klamath
rules across the border of Oregon and California—a deep green
cut through unglaciated, V-shaped river valleys that harbor ecosystems of world-class levels of biodiversity.

02. Iron Gate Dam, scheduled for removal by 2020.

03. Copco Dams 1 and 2, scheduled for removal by 2020.

04. John C. Boyle Dam, scheduled for removal by 2020. The
removal of these four hydroelectric dams is the largest dam

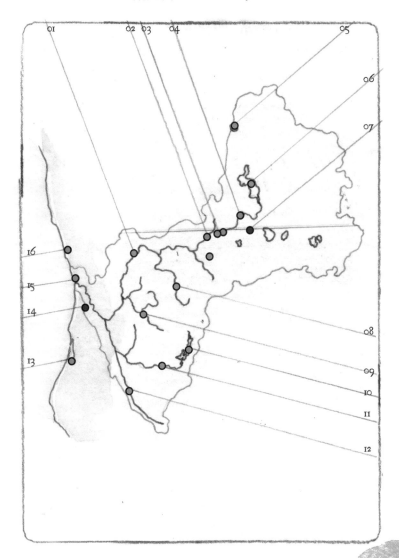

01 02 03 04 05 06 07 08 09 10 11 12 13 14 15 16

removal and salmon restoration effort in US history. Although the removal of the dams themselves may not be sufficient to immediately restore the connective health of the river mouth to its headwaters, this course of action is a high opportunity to reverse the path to extinction of Klamath salmon runs and to open our hearts and minds toward the reconciliation of ourselves with the natural world.

Black Skimmer
Rynchops niger

05. Crater Lake National Park.

06. Upper Klamath Lake.

07. California-Oregon border. Three of the dams slated for removal are south of the border and one is north.

08. Scott River.

09. Salmon River.

10. Trinity Reservoir (see map 01.01).

11. Trinity River. Trinity River water gives salmon in the struggling Klamath River below the confluence essential cold water, especially vital in drought years, although both rivers remain impaired by dams and diversions.

12. South Forth Trinity River.

13. Eureka (city).

14. Klamath River watershed, approximately 15,000 square miles. "Dam removal can rewrite a painful chapter in our history, and it can be done in a manner that protects the many interests in the Basin." Sally Jewell, Secretary of the Interior, US Department of the Interior, 2016.[4]

15. Klamath (town).

16. Crescent City.

North Siskiyou Mountains Salamander

Can we dig into nature without the everywhere handprint of humankind? How ingenuous the word, pristine! Everywhere trammeled. There is memory in wilderness and in memory, meaning. I don't find meaning in these new human place facsimiles. Sterile all, and full of emptiness. Give me community. Give me my family of life. Only biodiversity can give my heart its home.

Plethodon stormi

Northern Mountains

Siskiyou mountains Salamander

PART THREE:
SOUTHLAND WATER

Map 03.01

Replenishment of the Salton Sea

Tracking solutions for California's number-one mess

In 1905, the Salton Sink became the Salton Sea (California's largest lake by surface area) because of a two-year breach in the original canal from the Colorado River. The lake was only ever fifty feet deep and is now home to over four hundred species of birds.

It is shrinking, it is toxic, and it is a problem. In 2003, the Imperial Valley transferred 3.1 MAF of water allocations to San Diego County for drinking water. That means that the Imperial Valley can afford to upgrade their water efficiency and conservation strategies, but the Salton Sea will no longer be replenished by polluted agriculture runoff.[1] The clock is ticking: at the beginning of 2018 the Imperial Irrigation District cut off the flow of water from the Colorado River into the Salton Sea as required by this agreement.[2] It has been estimated that letting the Salton Sea further degrade into a bowl of toxic dust, left by evaporated fertilizers and pesticides, may cost California $70 billion in reduced values, health costs, and agricultural production lost.[3]

In 2017, Governor Jerry Brown unveiled a $400 million plan to restore thirty thousand of the fifty thousand wetland acres

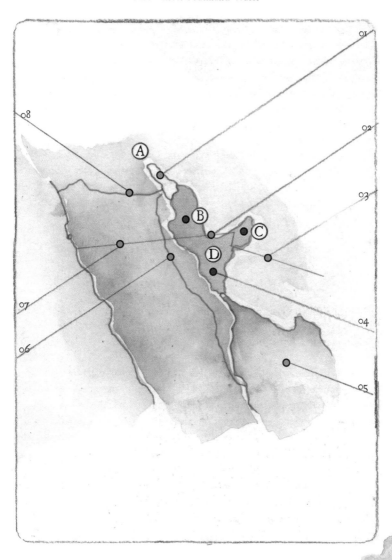

expected to dry up in the Salton Sea in the next ten years, but only budgeted $80 million.[4] It is an okay plan, but not a great one. There is a much better plan on the table to fix this: the sea-to-sea plan (outlined below, see 06. Gulf Restoration Pipeline). It will be expensive but it is a sustainable plan that will remediate the entire problem if we are bold enough to act on it. This is our state's most expensive mess.

A. Coachella Valley, including Palm Springs. Despite its surface aridity, the valley sits on a legally contentious groundwater supply of perhaps 30 MAF; .28 MAF is the average approximate annual delivery from the Colorado River to the Coachella Valley's 60,000 acres of farmland.[5]

B. Imperial Valley. A handful of landowners—about five hundred farms in all—control the rights to 3.1 million acre-feet a year from the Colorado River.[6]

C. Yuma, Arizona, water district.

D. Mexicali, agricultural region.

01. Salton Sea—the state's ten-year "band-aid" plan calls for construction of 29,800 acres of ponds, wetlands, and dust-suppression projects on portions of the exposed lake bed. The Salton Sea Management Program outlines annual targets for completion, beginning with 500 acres in 2018 and ramping up to 4,200 acres in 2028.[7] That leaves 60,000 acres of lake bed exposed to the desert winds. The damage to migratory bird habitat will be enormous and the potential remains of not being able to hold onto the foothold of wetlands restored, as they may be swallowed by an exponential increase in severe dust storms.[8]

02. Mexicali.

03. Arizona-Mexico border.

04. Colorado River Delta.

05. Gulf of California.

06. Gulf Restoration Pipeline (proposed route). The sea-to-sea solution: to raise and control the salinity of the Salton Sea, the plan is to infuse it with nearly .28 MAF of ocean water every year. Laguna Salada is a Mexican canal 25 miles from the Salton Sea and flows to the Sea of Cortez (40 miles). To expand the canal we need to negotiate a deal with Mexico, the cost is good at less than $1 billion.[9] To build a new canal we are looking at closer to $50 billion.[10]

07. California-Mexico border.

08. Pacific Restoration Pipeline (proposed route). If it turns out that the international negotiations required to create the Laguna Salada pipeline are prohibitive, plan B is to build a pipeline to the Pacific on this side of the border. The cost to build and maintain this pipeline would be significantly more at an estimated $3 billion, as this project will require multiple pumping stations to get the water over the Santa Rosa Mountains. The Pacific Restoration Pipeline would also require an estimated annual energy consumption of 1,000 GW.[11]

Southwestern Willow Flycatcher
Empidonax trailii extimus

Southwestern Willow Flycatcher

Reciprocation and gratitude, in the human ecol-
ogy, work to balance the necessary ratio between
extraction and replenishment of the more-than-
human world. This is a fundamental function of
how resilient communities grow into perpetuating
abundance. The endless commodification of our nat-
ural resources is a recipe for extinction, and exists
only because we feed on and are being sold the myth
of scarcity. A collective posture of gratitude, one
that involves giving back to the natural world and
its living systems, will always yield an economy of
plenty. The only way the people live is if we realize
we already have everything we need, because that
was the gift.

Map 03.02

Allocations on the Colorado

The denouement of the American Nile

In 1869, John Wesley Powell, a staunch and scientifically minded, one-armed veteran, was the first to successfully navigate the unknown power of the Southwest's mightiest river: the Colorado. Powell would later pen the ever-influential *Report on the Lands of the Arid Region of the United States* and become the director of the US Geologic Survey. His prescient knowledge of how water (or the lack of it) would determine development of the West would serve as a warning and a promise.

Powell was the first to clearly understand the nature of aridity across the West and saw that all life, political or otherwise, should be organized around water. "This, then, is the proposition I make: that the entire arid region be organized into natural hydrographic districts, each one to be a commonwealth within itself for the purpose of controlling and using the great values which have been pointed out. The plan is to establish local self-government by hydrographic basins."[1]

What if in the next one or two hundred years, when the lawns of twenty-first-century suburbia have been returned to steppe, to desert, and to xeriscape, when seniority rights for dwindling supplies of fresh water may fade into scorched, desiccated irrelevance, when even the most stringent and efficient conservation technologies of tomorrow are not enough to meet our needs, we might then come around to Powell's original idea of how to organize our society out here in the arid West? Whatever happens, the fate of the Colorado River will be in the middle of that debate for our future. Arguably,

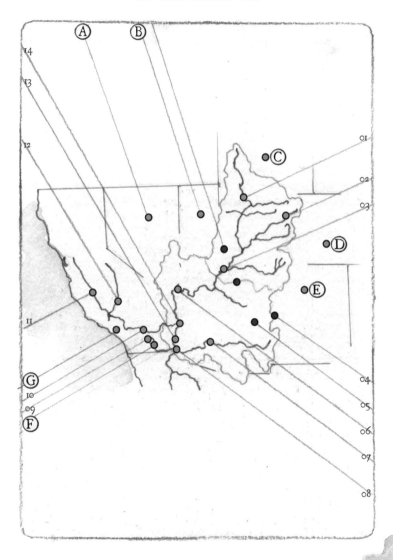

no watercourse in the world is more fought over or sustains more human life and economy than the West's greatest river, the Colorado.

In 1922, the estimated 15.00 MAF outflow of the Colorado River was apportioned out and California got 4.40 MAF.[2] Currently the Colorado flows at 12.4 MAF. It is quite the understatement to say that the predicted shortfall of 3.20 MAF by 2060 and the compounded per annum deficit of over 1.00 MAF due to reservoir evaporation imperil the future ability of the river to supply the seven states that depend on it with their negotiated allocations.[3] Few negotiations take root that might change allocations on the Colorado—too often, stubborn politicians would rather fight than compromise. The latest plan seems to have gained purchase: the Pilot Drought Response Actions Project between California, Arizona, and Nevada as negotiated by the Bureau of Reclamation has a goal of saving 1.5 million acre-feet of water by 2019.[4] The project approves and releases funds to applicants—individual citizens, industry, government, and others—who are building and planning water conservation infrastructure.

The fate of this overtaxed river will hang in the balance for the foreseeable future. For now, the Colorado does not reach its historic mouth in Mexico's Gulf of California. That is, of course, like all things in contemporary water culture, by design. With the signing of Minute 319 (2012), the Morellos Dam—the last dam on the Colorado—was opened for a one-time release in 2014. With this act, twenty-three miles from the dam, the Colorado reached the sea for the first time in sixteen years, and for a season the ancient delta was revivified.[5] Whether or not that will ever happen again remains to be seen.

A. Nevada. Negotiated .30 MAF (in 1928). Arizona got 2.80 MAF in the same deal.[6]

B. Utah. Negotiated 23% of the Upper Basin flow (in 1948).[7]

C. Wyoming. Negotiated 14% of the Upper Basin flow (in 1948).

D. Colorado. Negotiated 51.75% of the Upper Basin flow (in 1948).

E. New Mexico. Negotiated 11.25% of the Upper Basin flow (in 1948).

F. Imperial Irrigation District.

G. Metro Water District.

01. Green River.

02. Colorado River—1,450 miles long. With already a 15% on average decline in precipitation in the river basin in the first two decades of the twenty-first century, and based on the effects of climate change, more precipitation coming as rain, snowmelt coming earlier, and rising rates of reservoir evaporation, it is estimated that we are looking at a grand total reduction in river flow of upward of 50% by the end of the century.[8]

03. Lake Powell and Glen Canyon Dam. River: Colorado, (s) 24.32 MAF; FWP; (h) 1320 MW. Lake Powell serves the four Upper Basin states (Colorado, Utah, Wyoming, and New Mexico).

04. Colorado River watershed. The Colorado River Basin has warmed by 2°F in the last century and has endured sixteen years of drought.[9]

05. Lower Basin. Lake Mead serves the three Lower Basin states

(California, Arizona, and Nevada).

o6. Lake Mead and Hoover Dam. River: Colorado, (s) 26.13 MAF; FWP; (h) 2,080 MW of which California buys about 60%. Lake Mead now has a third straw at the 800-foot level. The lowest water level ever on the reservoir was recorded in 2016 at 1,074 feet. It was 100 feet higher twenty-five years ago.[10]

o7. Gila River.

o8. Yuma Project, Central Arizona Project.

o9. Salton Sea and the Coachella Valley Water District: along with the Imperial Irrigation District, allocated 3.85 MAF (1931).

10. Colorado River Aqueduct. In 2007 California renegotiated the seniority of its water rights—California is going to get its water. The state routinely takes more than its negotiated share.[11] The Metropolitan Water District of Southern California is allocated .55 MAF (1931).

11. California Aqueduct.

12. Los Angeles Aqueduct.

13. Palo Verde Irrigation District: allocated .30 MAF (1931).

14. Havasu Reservoir and Parker Dam. River: Colorado, (s) .62 MAF. Mohave Reservoir and Davis Dam, (s) .28 MAF.

bighorn drinking from the Colorado

California condor
Gymnogyps californianus

Part Three: Southland Water

Arroyo toad
Anaxyus californicus

Arroyo Toad

The parade of challenges before us and this desert, from within and without, is an easy course in despair. Indulging in such postures is not our luxury. Whether addressing a shrinking water table, water policy and conveyance itself, cripplingly expensive environmental remediation—tended to or not—or the machinations of bullying politicians and businessmen forwarding ecologically costly agendas, we shall push back, we shall abide. We shall do so because everywhere here we see treasure—its value glints off every yellow creosote flower and in the wealth of distant coyote song that we hold in our walking bones. In its unlimited grace, the Sonora Desert, bed of the California Colorado, welcomes our respect. We have the right to protect the desert and we have the responsibility to protect the desert.

PART FOUR:
A MOMENT OF RESTORATION

Map 04.01

Hetch Hetchy Revisited

The bravest of all opportunities

"These temple destroyers, devotees of ravaging commercialism, seem to have a perfect contempt for nature." —John Muir

I believe with all my heart that this project is the jewel in the crown of a new majestic day for California—the bravest opportunity to present to the whole world the gift of an emancipated Hetch Hetchy Valley as a symbol of who we are, as Californians, and in our most solemn posture to present a unity of identity— one that understands that all the rights we enjoy are met with equal responsibilities. Despite the daily tweeting of cold-hearted, corporate mouthpieces who sow conflict, we continue our march toward a new reality: a reality whereby we put aside some indulgences of consumerist modernity, with its artificial contrivances of the red versus blue disparity, and we take to investing in great acts of restoration. We will continue our state's legacy of standing up for what is right and doing what just makes plain, good sense.

I foresee O'Shaughnessy Dam breached in my lifetime. I see San Franciscans embracing the water security offered by an already augmented San Pedro Dam. In fact, the only true obstacle we have to realizing the vision of Hetch Hetchy Valley restored is a few

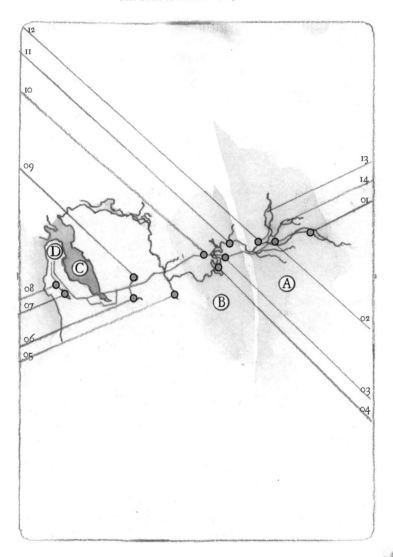

private corporations telling us negotiations are not possible. I see San Francisco reclaiming its title, its identity as a truly green city, perhaps the first historically self-identified green city. I see the National Park Service supporting a no-brainer investment toward a pending windfall with this newly uncovered treasure. Most importantly, in the restoration of Hetch Hetchy, I see the exciting work of hope kindled in a citizenry unafraid and un-shy to take back its legacy, uniting in a single voice to this keystone moment, indicative of even greater things to come.

A. The Sierra Nevada
B. The foothills
C. San Francisco Bay
D. The City and County of San Francisco

01. Hetch Hetchy Reservoir and the O'Shaughnessy Dam. Estimates to remove this unnecessary reservoir in the twin valley to Yosemite within the National Park range from $1 billion to $4 billion. It is safe to budget the smaller end of the range, as the higher end includes the building of more dams to offset the loss of this reservoir (which, studies have shown, won't be needed).[1] The tourist money will offset the cost of $1 billion to bring it down, making an estimated $9 billion from tourism in the first half century of restoration.[2]

02. Kirkwood Power Plant. San Francisco operates three medium-sized hydroelectric power plants in the Tuolumne River watershed. When O'Shaughnessy Dam is removed the total power delivered will decline from 400 MW to 350 MW. After the dam's removal, power at Kirkwood will be significantly diminished during late summer and fall. Removing O'Shaughnessy Dam reduces hydropower generation and reduces revenues by approximately $12 million per year.[3]

03. Moccasin Powerhouse. Power loss at this station can be compensated by reusing water from Holm Power Plant, directed through the Mountain Tunnel.[4]

04. Don Pedro Reservoir. In 1971, this principal reservoir on the Tuolumne River was increased in capacity from .29 MAF to 2.03 MAF. The mean annual flow of the Tuolumne River in total is 2.00 MAF. Without storage at Hetch Hetchy, San Francisco would still derive most of its water supply from the Tuolumne River. Constructing a new intertie at or below Don Pedro Reservoir would allow the city to have access to its supplies in the reservoir.[5]

05. San Joaquin River.

06. Calaveras Reservoir and Dam. River: Arroyo Hondo, (s) .10 MAF; (p) LWP; Santa Clara County; seismically vulnerable dam.

07. Crystal Springs Reservoir and Dam. River: San Mateo Creek, (s) .06 MAF; (p) LWP; San Mateo County.

08. San Andreas Reservoir and Dam. River: San Andreas Creek, (s) .02 MAF; (p) LWP; San Mateo County.

09. San Antonio Reservoir and Turner Dam. River: San Antonio Creek, (s) .05 MAF; (p) LWP; Alameda County.

10. Hetch Hetchy System Pipeline.

11. Tuolumne River.

12. Holm Power Plant. Tuolumne's third power plant. Power output will be unaffected by removal of the dam.

13. Cherry Reservoir. River: Cherry Creek, (s) .27 MAF; (p) LWP.

14. Eleanor Reservoir. River: Eleanor Creek, (s) .26 MAF; (p) LWP. The other reservoir in the park owned and operated by San Francisco.

Hetch Hetchy Valley restored

Hetch Hetchy

It has been a hundred years
that my heart was buried
in the still water.
Every evening at sunset
I see a thousand cranes rise
from the reservoir and on their wings,
the valley empties.
In the morning,
the bears dream of their return
with sapphire eyes uncut on salmon's tooth.
In a thousand years, the liquid granite
will begin to forget the thirst stains
marring the holy bowl
across the outstretched song of the river,
beneath the arboreal pulse
of the restored place
that was meant for sky, not flood.

North american River otter
Lontra canadensis

The Otter

*The next several hundred years will be the age of ecology.
We will learn how remediation becomes restoration and
moves to stewardship for the conservation and preservation
of biosphere system balances that make human life possible.
Since the late eighteenth century, when we entered the era
of the carbon economy and began the veiling of the whole
surface of the planet in a thin layer of combustion's residue,
then again in 1945 when we upped the ante on the process
and deposited another layer of strata in the form of radio-
active particles that marked the beginning of humanity's
nuclear age, we entered a new, geologically detectable age of
the Holocene, the Anthropocene, or as E. O. Wilson warns,
the age of loneliness. If in fact it is to be an age of loneliness,
the so-called sixth massive extinction that is proceeding at
a rate corresponding directly with the exponential growth of
our species, we will only witness its beginnings and not its
far-reaching effects. Our existence is supported by a network
of all life that reaches to touch all pieces of the biosphere.
With collective vision, we are together drawing another path
through this labyrinth, one that is at least locally alive more
now than it was fifty years ago. From this context, a painting
of a river otter is far more than just a cute aquatic predator
regaining a foothold—it is a symbol of us, recognizing the
way to our future legacy by examining, supporting, and
reinforcing the legacy of nature's past. As much habitat as
we can return to wild, endemic patterns is investment in our
own rich and resilient future.*

PART FIVE:
PATTERNS IN CONSERVATION

05.a. The Future of Human-Water Ecology

Water in California is not like water anywhere else. Nowhere else on the planet has so much been done with so little of the precious substance. Nowhere else on the planet has it been moved so far, over mountains to transform deserts, feeding what would become the modern nation's number-one agricultural producing region.

Water means everything everywhere—water means life. To dominate the distribution of water is to dominate all life. In just over one hundred years, we've worked to manicure all aspects of the waterscape. We've worked to curate and control every drop saved and spent. We've also willingly sacrificed aspects of a natural legacy, swaths of living, wild California bartered for industrialized civilization. Far from despair, we are now waking up to an opportunity for a reimagining of our relationship to how, when, where, and even why we store, convey, and use water. We made a deal: trade a natural legacy for unprecedented agriculture and the richest cities in the world. The bill has come due and we need to rapidly renegotiate the contract. Fortunately, the tools we need are already laid on the table. Run the math and the numbers reveal that we have enough water. Even in the face of climate change and an ever-growing population, we have enough water. What we find ourselves short on is unified vision, and willingness to transform, compromise, and conserve.

05.b. Agricultural Use, by the Numbers

California agriculture accounts for just over 4 percent of the state's economic output, just under 4 percent of total jobs, and adds about 3 percent to its total value.[1] Across California's 100 million total acres, 43 million are used for agriculture—16 million acres for grazing and 27 million for cropland,[2] 9 million of which are irrigated.[3] Agriculture in the San Joaquin and Sacramento Valleys depends on the delivery of water from the State Water Project and the Central Valley Project. Agricultural irrigation swings between using 40 percent of all of California's available water upward to 80 percent depending on rainfall and legal minimums for environmental flow in rivers.[4] Regardless of percentages, as it is configured right now, California agriculture needs between 33 and 37 MAF of water per year—what isn't delivered by aqueduct is taken out of the ground.[5]

Of the forty-five different primary crops grown in California, only four use nearly one third of all the water used for agriculture. The thirsty four are alfalfa (used mainly to feed livestock), nuts (almonds, pistachios, and others), rice (mostly exported), and cotton, which collectively use 10 MAF of water per year and with a collective area of 2.9 million acres take up about a third of all of California's irrigated farmland.[6] Alfalfa, a perennial crop (which means you don't need to plant it every year), is farmed on over 900,000 acres and uses 5 MAF/year.[7] At 1.1 million acres, there's twice as much almond acreage in California as there was two decades ago.[8] Rice is grown over approximately 500,000 acres. Although it may seem strange that rice, which requires flood irrigation, is grown in California, it does very well with California's climate and soil. And now, to complicate matters, alfalfa and rice fields provide habitat for many endangered species, including 40 percent of the world's remaining populations of tricolored blackbirds,[9] and rice fields provide nutrients for young salmon on their way to the sea. Although you save 1.20 acre-feet of water per acre growing wheat compared to growing cotton,[10] cotton is still popular in California because of its incredibly high yield compared to other areas where it is planted. Because of the profitability of almonds and other nuts now encroaching on fields historically planted with cotton, cotton acreage has dwindled to about 400,000 acres from 1.3 million acres.

The fight for an ever more water-efficient agricultural industry in California will never end. With decreasing intervals between drought events and an increasing population, the stakes are now higher than they've ever been. Upgrading agricultural techniques (evaluating how much water to apply—consider the California Irrigation Management System)[11] and infrastructure (using state money to improve technologies—consider the State Water Efficiency and Enhancement Program)[12] is a challenge that is being tackled head-on. We are investing in an overhaul of irrigation efficiency technology (no more flooding, only sprinkler, drip, and subsurface), regulating irrigation deficits (applying less water), and improving irrigation scheduling (applying precision science to watering calendars).[13] By using these techniques we can, in a dry year, conserve an estimated 6 million acre-feet of water.[14] That is two Shasta Reservoirs' worth of water.

05.c. Urban Use, by the Numbers

If Los Angeles had never diverted the Owens River, dooming Owens Lake to terminal desiccation, and did not still negotiate huge quantities of imported water from the California Aqueduct (from the Sacramento, Trinity, and American Rivers) and from the Colorado River, it might never have exceeded the natural capacity of an estimated human population of five hundred thousand.[1]

In 1930, six years after Owens Lake was turned to dust by the faraway city, Los Angeles' population at 1.2 million surpassed San Francisco's for the first time. Today the population is 3.8 million, and with no plentiful surface water source of its own, the city imports nearly 88 percent (.55 MAF) of its water. In only fifteen years, that number will fall to 57 percent (.41 MAF) as Los Angeles begins to realize a massive plan that includes upping the amount of groundwater being pumped from .07 MAF to .11 MAF, upping the amount of recycled water used for municipal irrigation from .01 MAF to .06 MAF, and meeting strict conservation goals of .06 MAF. All this while increasing the amount of water used by the city by 12 percent in accordance with population growth.[2]

This kind of redistribution of water assets and resetting the strategy from multiple angles is essential for municipalities everywhere to plan for in the face of climate change and population growth. The most amazing thing happened in 2015 when we had one of the driest years in California history: our cities hit their conservation goals of 25 percent. In one season, we pulled together and saved one half million acre-feet of water, because of which we saved 1830 GWh (gigawatt hours) of electricity (water is the biggest single electricity customer in our state)[3], and because of that, we then reduced CO_2 emissions by half a million tons—the equivalent of taking 110,000 cars off the road for the whole year.[4] This is just the beginning of what we can do.

As the population has been increasing, California urban water use has been going down. Per capita water use declined significantly—from 232 gallons per day in 1995 to 178 gallons per day in 2010.[5] This is probably due mostly to incentivizing water-use technology, such as efficient showers and toilets, but also from a greater, popular awareness of drought conditions and our arid state. If we

The Grizzly Bear

New paradigms reveal themselves as revolutions—
fundamental shifts in the way humans organize and
govern themselves and their resources. The three major
historical revolutions that have determined our course
as the world-changing species that we are have been the
cognitive, the agricultural, and the industrial. One way
or another, we will soon be ensconced in the fourth great
paradigm shift: the ecological. We will realize and thrive
in a new worldview, or it will be a time of unilateral
destruction. I certainly don't mean to offer some doom
and gloom prophecy nor do I want to necessarily echo the
end-times scenarios that some have described for decades.
My concern is with the linguistic and pictorial mech-
anisms that trigger the deepest shifts in our collective
psyche. Is it possible to clear the fog of alienation from
the natural world that has plagued urban society for so
many thousands of years? I think the possibility is there
and I have found an orientation through this dense forest.
It is a simpler path than you might think, dependent on
a linguistic determinism, or how the words people use
determine the way people think.

California Grizzly bear, extinct
Ursus arctos californicus

continue this trend to a very possible, yet staggeringly low goal of thirty-two gallons per person per day (18 percent of today's standard) and if residential use continues to account for 64 percent of urban usage, which averages 9.10 MAF today but will increase by 12 percent (per Los Angeles' water plan) to 10.40 MAF, we will attain a net annual conservation of 1.11 MAF from what we use today, even with the expected population increase of over twenty million people in the next twenty years.[6]

This solution, a hyperconservative, water-efficient society, is so appealing because it is a trajectory we are already on. While it may mean the end of some traditions (lawns, for example), great strides can be made simply with less waste in our daily lives, and we are not just talking about direct water conservation. Take for instance food: Californians throw away nearly six million tons of food scraps or food waste each year, roughly 25 percent of all food grown, or approximately nine million acre-feet of water.[7] With food waste laws now becoming a reality, the amount of water savings implicit in their enforcement is remarkable.[8]

05.d. The Wisdom of Future Water Projects

Over the past 170 years, we've successfully duped ourselves into believing that a huge chunk of the West is something other than an arid steppe. We are now entering an era when the building of federally funded big dams is through. There are a few projects still on the books, most notably Sites Reservoir in the Sacramento Valley, Centennial Dam on the Bear River, and Temperance Flat just behind Friant on the San Joaquin. To further pursue such projects may not be in line with our best interests.[1] For those of us who study California water and California climate, the next hundred years are going to go one way, and new water projects are not going to help.[2] If the rain doesn't fall, more storage does not mean more water. Next to what I've already shown as to what we can save by conservation alone, these new water projects are our most expensive option.[3]

With at least one major reservoir on every river that eventually makes its diminished way to the Sacramento–San Joaquin Delta, we have already built more than adequate storage. If there were no diversions at all, across the biggest twenty-four rivers with dams currently collecting their water (all of them exist in the Sacramento and San Joaquin Valleys), the outflow (into the delta) would average 29.68 MAF. As it is, the storage capacity on those rivers is approximately 31.30 MAF.[4] California's current total surface water storage capacity is over 40 MAF. The twentieth-century infrastructure is now aged, and it is being challenged by emerging patterns of long drought followed by times of deluge. The Oroville Dam crisis of 2017 was an excellent and terrifying example of the paramount need to inventory the readiness of the entire system.[5] Instead of building new water projects, our money would be better spent repairing our existing system and even identifying projects that can go, working always to restore the legacy of California's natural world and seeing more jobs doing it than building new projects.[6]

A dam may appear in our minds to be permanent, a monument to the ages, when dams are, of course, structures that can be redesigned or removed if we will it so. Since 1950, sixty-seven dams have been removed because of safety concerns, for the restoration of riparian habitat, to improve fish passage, for erosion control, to enhance recreational opportunities, because the dam failed, for the removal of invasive bullfrog breeding sites, and for flood control.[7] In the previous two sections, I made the case for conservation as the single greatest tool we have in our strategy toward California's water future. Preparing for a warmer and drier climate and its implications for California water usage has afforded us this strategy on how we can preserve agriculture in the Central Valley and our lifestyle in the urban centers, while working to restore the natural fecundity of the returning wild paradise.

05.e. Conservation Summary

When it comes to water in the future, there is one word to think about, to sing from the mountaintops and to implement into regular practice above all other policies: conservation. The aging dams are filling with silt, and building more dams won't help.[1] With less precipitation and already an excess of storage, they will never fill.[2] The old refrains of the twentieth century calling for more storage aren't viable as they don't account for the coming of a possible megadrought,[3] they trade limited success for huge expense,[4] and they deny the utilization of existing technology and practices as a priority.[5] Water use stands on three legs—a

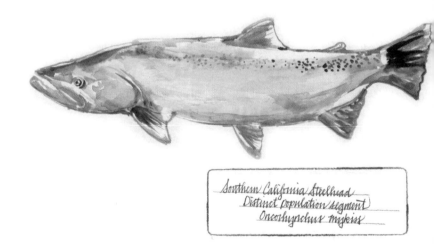

Southern California Steelhead
Distinct population segment
Oncorhynchus mykiss

tripod of dependency that the waterscape of California supports: agriculture, municipalities, and the environment. Only by rethinking policies and tools that we already have can we ensure our continued human residency over the next few hundred years with a continued, generalized sense of peace and prosperity.

Modern California uses about 40 MAF in a year, 67 percent of it from surface water.[6] In the agricultural sector, we have estimated that we could save upward of 6 MAF.[7] In metropolitan (urban) usage, we have a per capita saving of 25 percent, another .50 MAF,[8] water-saving technologies upgrades from 1.11 to a potential 1.5 MAF with another potential five million acre-feet with local storm water capture and recycling.[9] Without including emerging technologies (such as green, industrial-scale desalinization and groundwater recharge projects), we are now looking at future usage approaching less than 30 MAF. Most of our plans to create a resilient water supply consistent with our environmental values are so often stymied by state-level gridlock. Bureaucratic infighting, budget constraints, and the record-breaking drought become dwarfed by our biggest obstacle: trusting each other. But I am sure we are up for it: we are Californians and there is one thing that we have shown again and again and that is our love of a good challenge.

My life as a mapmaker of California's living world leans toward systems organization and not resource utility. The future resiliency and existence of our human society depend on not only defending biodiversity (and the living systems that support that biodiversity) from habitat loss, but restoring vast tracts of lost habitat in the form of wildlife connectivity bridges between currently protected areas. Ensuring the continued ability of the living networks that support and feed every level of the natural world, and that have been systematically denigrated for over 170 years, is where we should focus our policies of development and resource allocation. Striking the balance between extraction and replenishment and replacing the idea of reclamation with the vision of restoration will be the work of the next several generations to come. For now, our job is to participate in a greater responsibility of geographic literacy and to debate how the tangled interface of private and public land works to serve or hinder our legacy and the natural health of the state, and thereby ourselves.

We are talking about moving rivers—deep, long-cut entrenchments in the most incalcitrant landscapes of our society—and moving rivers takes time. One day you find that your maps are outdated, that public paradigms have pushed the old fences out to dysfunction, and we are then made free to enjoy the new freedoms of a restored landscape, both inner and outer, to move toward our relationship with each other, with the land, and toward both the past and the future.

Obi Kaufmann

Winter 2018
Oakland, California

Notes

Epigraph. 1. Kalahari proverb, quoted in James R. Workman, *Heart of Dryness: How the Last Bushmen Can Help Us Endure the Coming Age of Permanent Drought* (New York: Bloomsbury, 2009). This is the paradox at the core of my presentation. In California, we most certainly do govern water and the relationship between our power over it and its power over us is central to any vision of the future.

Introduction

1. US Department of the Interior, National Park Service, "Water in the West," www.nps.gov/articles/2-water-in-the-west.htm (accessed June 15, 2018).

2. Pacific Institute, "Urban Water Conservation and Efficiency Potential in California" (2011), 2, www.Pacinst.org.

PART ONE: THE BIG PICTURE
Map 01.01 Water Yesterday, Water Today, Water Tomorrow

1. Sarah Gilman, "This will be the biggest dam removal project in history," https://news.nationalgeographic.com/2016/04/160411-klamath -glen-canyon-dam-removal-video-anniversary (accessed June 15, 2018).

2. Ryan Sabalow and Dale Kasler, "This one stretch of river could decide the future of Shasta Dam," www.sacbee.com/news/state /california/water-and-drought/article209471359.html (accessed June 15, 2018).

3. Ryan Sabalow, "Groups file first legal challenges in Delta tunnels fight," www.sacbee.com/news/state/california/water-and-drought /delta/article158897079.html (accessed June 15, 2018).

4. Sierra Nevada Conservancy, "California's Primary Watershed," www.sierranevada.ca.gov/our-region/ca-primary-watershed (accessed June 15, 2018).

5. Water Education Foundation, "Looking to the Source: Watersheds of the Sierra Nevada," www.sierranevada.ca.gov/our-region/docs /waterreport.pdf (accessed June 15, 2018).

6. David Carle, *Water and the California Dream* (Berkeley: Counterpoint, 2016), 211–15.

7. Todd Fitchette, "Subsidence shrinks Friant-Kern Canal capacity by 60 percent," www.westernfarmpress.com/irrigation-systems/subsidence -shrinks-friant-kern-canal-capacity-60-percent (accessed June 15, 2018).

8. Los Angeles Department of Water and Power, "Urban Water Management Plan" (2010), exhibit ES-B, LADWP Historical Water Supply Sources 1980–2010.

9. Marc Reisner, *Cadillac Desert* (New York: Penguin, 1986), chapter 4, "American Nile."

10. Jonathan Overpeck and Brad Udall, "Climate Change and the Colorado River: What We Already Know," October 2016, www. coloradoriverresearchgroup.org/uploads/4/2/3/6/42362959/crrg _climate_change.pdf.

11. San Diego State University, "The Salton Sea: A Brief Description of Its Current Conditions, and Potential Remediation Projects" (1997), www.sci.sdsu.edu/salton/Salton%20Sea%20Description.html (accessed June 15, 2018).

12. Los Angeles Department of Water and Power, "Urban Water Management Plan" (2010), exhibit ES-Q, LADWP Historical Water Supply Sources 1980–2010.

13. Los Angeles Department of Water and Power, "Urban Water Management Plan" (2010), exhibit ES-Q, LADWP Historical Water Supply Sources 1980–2010.

14. California Environmental Protection Agency, Air Resources Board, *Staff Report: ARB Review of State Implementation Plan for Owens Valley* (2016), www.arb.ca.gov/planning/sip/planarea/gbasin/owens/staff _report_2016owens.pdf.

15. Los Angeles Department of Water and Power, "Urban Water Management Plan" (2010), exhibit ES-Q, LADWP Historical Water Supply Sources 1980–2010.

16. Mark Arax and Rick Wartzman, *The King of California* (New York: Public Affairs, 2003), 184–93.

17. San Joaquin River Restoration Program, www.restoresjr.net /restoration-flows/, 2016 (accessed August 20, 2018). Josh Newcom, "After 60 years, Chinook salmon spawn in San Joaquin River," www. usbr.gov/newsroom/stories/detail.cfm?RecordID=61547 (accessed June 15, 2018).

18. Spreck Rosekrans, "Restoration of Hetch Hetchy Valley and San Francisco's Water Supply," www.sierracollege.edu/ejournals/jsnhb /v6n1/rosekrans.html (accessed June 15, 2018).

19. Sarah Null, "Water Supply Reliability Tradeoffs between Removing Reservoir Storage and Improving Water Conveyance in California," https://onlinelibrary.wiley.com/doi/full/10.1111/1752-1688.12391 (2016) (accessed June 15, 2018).

20. San Francisco Public Utilities Commission, 2015 Urban Water Management Plan (June 2016), San Francisco Water Power Sewer, for the City and County of San Francisco, www.sfwater.org/Modules /ShowDocument.aspx?documentID=8839 (accessed June 15, 2018).

21. Gary Snyder, *Mountains and Rivers Without End* (Berkeley: Counterpoint, 1996).

22. David Rains Wallace, *The Klamath Knot* (Berkeley: University of California Press), 1983.

23. See SB-5 California Drought, Water, Parks, Climate, Coastal Protection, and Outdoor Access For All Act of 2018. https://leginfo .legislature.ca.gov/faces/billNavClient.xhtml?bill_id=201720180SB5.

24. Food and Agriculture Organization of the United Nations, *Review of World Water Resources by Country*, "2. Concepts and Definitions; Groundwater concepts," 2003 (FAO/BRGM, 1996), www.fao .org/docrep/005/y4473e/y4473e06.htm (accessed June 15, 2018).

25. Local Government Commission, "'Banking' on Nature to Replenish Our Groundwater Supplies," www.lgc.org/resources/community -design/lpu/jul2015 (accessed June 15, 2018).

26. Friant Water Authority, "Subsidence Lowers Friant-Kern Canal by 5 inches in 5 months," www.friantwater.org/waterline/2017/11/30 /subsidence-lowers-friant-kern-canal-by-5-inches-in-5-months (accessed August 20, 2018).

Map 01.02 The Wild California Riverscape

1. National Wild and Scenic Rivers System, California, www.rivers .gov/california.php (accessed June 15, 2018).

2. Wild and Scenic Rivers Coordinating Council, technical report, "The Wild and Scenic River Study Process" (1999), US Forest Service and National Park Service, Portland, Oregon and Anchorage, Alaska, www.rivers.gov/documents/study-process.pdf.

3. Statistics source: National Wild and Scenic Rivers System, California, www.rivers.gov/california.php (accessed June 15, 2018).

4. American Rivers, "Rogue and Smith Rivers," www.americanrivers .org/river/rogue-and-smith-rivers/ (accessed June 15, 2018).

5. US Department of the Interior, National Marine Fisheries Service, "Klamath Dam Removal Overview Report for the Secretary of the Interior" (2013), https://klamathrestoration.gov/sites/klamathrestoration .gov/files/Full%20SDOR%20accessible%20022216.pdf.

6. US Bureau of Reclamation, "Shasta/Trinity River Division Project," www.usbr.gov/projects/index.php?id=342 (accessed June 15, 2018).

7. "Cannabis is a thirsty plant, and with the increased use of water to supply a growing industry, many communities have witnessed the effects of impaired watersheds. The pumping of water during dry summer months can leave salmonids and other water-bound animals without any chance for survival and may be pushing local species such as coho salmon to the brink of extinction." Kyle Keegan, "North Coast Living," Trees Foundation, *Forest & River News* (December 2011), www.treesfoundation.org/publications/article-476.

Map 01.03, California's Water Projects

1. California's effective Gross Domestic Product as of 2018 is approximately $2.75 trillion, fifth in the world compared to all nations (www .bea.gov/newsreleases/regional/gdp_state/qgdpstate_newsrelease.htm). California is one of Conservation.org's top forty biodiversity hotspots and one of the earth's ten most endangered (www.conservation.org /NewsRoom/pressreleases/Pages/The-Worlds-10-Most-Threatened -Forest-Hotspots.aspx).

2. "Water right allocations total 400 billion cubic meters, approximately five times the state's mean annual runoff." Theodore Grantham and Joshua H. Viers, "100 years of California's Water rights system: patterns, trends and uncertainty" (2014), https://watershed.ucdavis .edu/files/biblio/WaterRights_UCDavis_study.pdf.

3. Glen M. MacDonald, Katrina A. Moser, et al., "Prolonged California aridity linked to climate warming and Pacific sea surface temperature" (2016), www.nature.com, www.nature.com/articles/srep33325.

4. "39% of state residents cited water/drought as the most pressing issue in May 2015, ahead of the jobs and the economy at 20%." Mitch Tobin, "Californians troubled by water and drought" (2016), Public Policy Institute of California, https://waterpolls.org/ppic-poll-water -drought/ (accessed June 15, 2018).

5. California Department of Water Resources, "2009 Comprehensive Water Package, Special Session Policy Bills and Bond Summary," www.water.ca.gov/LegacyFiles/legislation/docs/01272010waterpackage .pdf.

6. "Any long term plan of water sustainability in California will include, in addition to traditional hydrological sources, a portfolio of innovative water sources including recycling, desalinization, and most importantly conservation." California Department of Water Resources, "Integrated Regional Water Management," www.water .ca.gov/Programs/Integrated-Regional-Water-Management.

7. Stanford Woods Institute for the Environment, Water in the West, "Groundwater vs. Surface Water Storage Capacity," https://waterin thewest.stanford.edu/groundwater/charts/capacity-comparison/index .html (accessed June 15, 2018). The report puts the number at closer to 50 MAF.

8. Legislative Analyst's Office, State Water Resources Control Board, "Residential Water Use Trends and Implications for Conservation Policy" (2016), www.lao.ca.gov/Publications/Report/3611 (accessed June 15, 2018).

9. Union of Concerned Scientists, "California's Renewables Portfolio Standard (RPS) Program" (2016), www.ucsusa.org/sites/default/files /attach/2016/07/california-renewables-portfolio-standard-program .pdf (accessed June 15, 2018).

10. California Energy Commission, "California Hydroelectric Statistics & Data" www.energy.ca.gov/almanac/renewables_data/hydro (accessed June 15, 2018).

11. Warren Cornwall, "Hundreds of new dams could mean trouble for our climate" (2016), www.sciencemag.org/news/2016/09/hundreds -new-dams-could-mean-trouble-our-climate (accessed June 15, 2018).

12. Charles N. Alpers and Jacob A. Fleck, "Mercury transport and bioaccumulation in California reservoirs affected by historical gold mining," US Geological Survey, https://ca.water.usgs.gov/highlights /docs/USGS-Hg-reservoirs-webinar-1_Alpers-et-al_public.pdf (accessed June 15, 2018).

13. Metropolitan Water District of Southern California, "State Water Project, Sources of Supply" (2017), www.mwdh2o.com/AboutYour Water/Sources%20Of%20Supply/Pages/Imported.aspx (accessed June 15, 2018).

14. California Department of Water Resources, State Water Project, www.water.ca.gov/Programs/State-Water-Project (accessed June 15, 2018).

15. Friends of the River, "Sacramento Threat" Fact Sheet, 2016, Sites Project, www.friendsoftheriver.org/our-work/rivers-under-threat /sacramento-threat (accessed June 15, 2018).

16. Glen Martin, "No Joy in Mudville: Amid Drought, California's Reservoirs Are Clogged with Gunk" (2014), *California Magazine*, https://ced.berkeley.edu/events-media/news/no-joy-in-mudville -amid-drought-californias-reservoirs-are-clogged-with-gun (accessed June 15, 2018).

PART TWO: THE NORTHERN RIVERS
Map 02.01 Salmon and the Sacramento

1. Fourteen different runs, or evolutionarily significant units. University of California, Davis, "California Fish Species," http://calfish .ucdavis.edu/species (accessed August 20, 2018).

2. Federal Wildlife Service, "Pacific Salmon (*Oncorhynchus spp.*)," www.fws.gov/species/species_accounts/bio_salm.html (accessed August 20, 2018).

3. Noble Hendrix et al. (www.noaa.gov), "Life cycle modeling framework for Sacramento River winter-run Chinook salmon" (2014), https://swfsc.noaa.gov/publications/TM/SWFSC/NOAA-TM -NMFS-SWFSC-530.pdf (accessed Aug 20, 2018).

4. Lauren Sommer, "San Francisco Is Fighting California's Plan to Save Salmon. Wait. What?" www.kqed.org/science/1929999/san -francisco-is-fighting-californias-plan-to-save-salmon-wait-what, 2018 (accessed Aug 20, 2018).

5. California Department of Fish and Wildlife, CDFW Fish Hatcheries, www.wildlife.ca.gov/fishing/hatcheries (accessed June 15, 2018).

6. California Department of Fish and Wildlife, Threatened and Endangered Fish, www.dfg.ca.gov/wildlife/nongame/t_e_spp/fish .html (accessed June 15, 2018).

7. California Department of Water Resources, "Prospect Island Restoration Report" (2017), https://water.ca.gov/LegacyFiles /environmentalservices/docs/frpa/Prospect_DEIR_08_09_2016_Web .pdf (accessed June 15, 2018).

8. Sacramento River Watershed Program, "Sunflower Coordinated Resource Management Program," www.sacriver.org/aboutwatershed /roadmap/projects/sunflower-coordinated-resource-management -program (accessed June 15, 2018).

9. Sacramento River Watershed Program, "Iron Mountain Mine Superfund Cleanup," www.sacriver.org/aboutwatershed/roadmap /projects/iron-mountain-mine-superfund-cleanup (accessed June 15, 2018).

10. Alastair Bland, "For California Salmon, Drought and Warm Water Mean Trouble," *Yale Environment 360*, Yale School of Forestry and Environmental Studies, https://e360.yale.edu/features/for_california _salmon_drought_and_warm_water_mean_trouble?utm_source=folwd .com (accessed June 15, 2018).

11. Michelaina Johnson, "Cosumnes River Provides Model for Flood-plain Restoration in California" (2017), *Water Deeply*, www.newsdeeply .com/water/articles/2017/04/19/cosumnes-river-provides-model -for-floodplain-restoration-in-california (accessed June 15, 2018).

12. National Ocean and Atmospheric Administration, NOAA Fisheries, "Chinook Salmon (*Oncorhynchus tshawytscha*)," www.fisheries.noaa.gov /species/chinook-salmon (accessed June 15, 2018).

13. California Department of Fish and Wildlife, "California Department of Fish and Wildlife 2017 Salmon Information Meeting," https://nrm.dfg.ca.gov/FileHandler.ashx?DocumentID=14007.

Map 02.02 Restoration of the San Joaquin

1. Friant Water Authority, "Water Resources, Water Supply History and Update," https://friantwater.org/friant-water-resources (accessed June 15, 2018).

2. Water Education Foundation, "Mendota Pool," www.watereducation .org/aquapedia/mendota-pool (accessed June 15, 2018).

3. San Joaquin River Restoration Program, "First time in over 60 years: spring-run Chinook salmon spawn in the San Joaquin" (2017), www.restoresjr.net/seasonal-fish-monitoring-gets-underway (accessed June 15, 2018).

4. University of California, Davis, Agriculture and Natural Resources, Agricultural Issues Center, "Measure of California Agriculture" (2009), Aic.ucdavis.edu; http://aic.ucdavis.edu/publications/moca/mocamenu.htm.

5. California Department of Fish and Wildlife, California Endangered Species Act: "The Legislature directs the State (Fish and Game Code Section 2052) to conserve, protect, restore, and enhance any endangered species or any threatened species and its habitat, and it is the intent of the Legislature, consistent with conserving the species, to acquire lands for habitat for these species." www.wildlife.ca.gov/Conservation/CESA/FESA.

6. Lewis Griswold, "Temperance Flat Dam scores a big, fat zero from the state. Project's boosters are shocked," *Fresno Bee*, www.fresnobee.com/news/local/water-and-drought/article196955739.html (accessed June 15, 2018).

7. Rita Schmidt Sudman and Gary Pitzer, "The Friant Decision and the Future of the San Joaquin River" (2004), Water Education Foundation, www.watereducation.org/western-water-excerpt/friant-decision-and-future-san-joaquin-river (accessed June 15, 2018).

8. Billboards paid for by Families Protecting the Valley, familiesprotectingthevalley.com.

9. California Natural Resources Agency, California Water Fix, www.californiawaterfix.com.

10. The Peripheral Canal Act of 1982, https://ballotpedia.org/California_Proposition_9,_the_Peripheral_Canal_Act_(June_1982).

11. With Westlands Irrigation District balking at the price tag, the Central Valley Project is out of the deal, leaving only the State Water Project and the Metropolitan Water District (Los Angeles) in on the deal. See: Ryan Sabalow and Dale Kasler, "Farming district says it won't pay for Delta tunnels in a vote that could kill the project"

(September 2017), www.sacbee.com/news/state/california/water-and
-drought/delta/article174229771.html (accessed June 15, 2018).

12. The reverse backflow that supplies the Mendota Canal is a key
piece of infrastructure leading to the demise of many species, including the endangered delta smelt. See Glen Martin, "Bay Area / Smelt
decline turns off delta water pumps / Official says users relying on
state project will be OK." www.sfgate.com/bayarea/article/BAY-AREA
-Smelt-decline-turns-off-delta-water-2590298.php (accessed June 15,
2018).

13. California Natural Resources Agency, "California Eco Restore, a
Stronger Delta Ecosystem," http://resources.ca.gov/ecorestore
/what-is-california-ecorestore (accessed June 15, 2018).

14. California Waterfix, "A Modern Infrastructure Upgrade, Overview Fact Sheet" www.californiawaterfix.com/resources/fact-sheets
(accessed June 15, 2018).

15. Emily Green, "Sorry, my fellow environmentalists, we have to
build the tunnels," *Los Angeles Times*, www.latimes.com/opinion
/op-ed/la-oe-green-delta-tunnels-20171010-story.html (accessed June
15, 2018).

16. Restore the Delta, "There's a better solution to the Delta Tunnels," www.restorethedelta.org/theres-a-better-solution-to-ca-water
fix-delta-tunnels (accessed June 15, 2018).

Map 02.03 Emancipation of the Klamath

1. John Bezdak, "Decommissioning dams on the Klamath River to
restore resilience and long-term river, community health"(2016), US
Department of the Interior, www.doi.gov/blog/decommissioning
-dams-klamath-river-restore-resilience-and-long-term-river
-community-health (accessed June 15, 2018).

2. Oregon Wild, "Klamath River Water Quality," www.oregonwild
.org/waters/klamath/the-klamath-river/klamath-river-water-quality
(accessed June 15, 2018).

3. "Klamath River Basin: Overuse of river's resources is hurting farmers,
fishermen, tribes, and wildlife," www.klamathbasin.info
/CWC10mostendangered.pdf.

4. Sally Jewell, Secretary of the Interior, US Department of the
Interior, letter to the Federal Energy Regulatory Commission to
remove the Dams on the Klamath River (October 12, 2016), www.doi
.gov/sites/doi.gov/files/uploads/10_17_16_interior_letter_to_ferc.pdf.

PART THREE: SOUTHLAND WATER
Map 03.01 Replenishment of the Salton Sea

1. Imperial Irrigation District, "QSA—Water Transfer," www.iid.com
/water/library/qsa-water-transfer (accessed June 15, 2018).

2. Tyler Hayden, "How do we save the Salton Sea?" (2016), www
.audubon.org/magazine/summer-2016/how-do-we-save-salton-sea
(accessed June 15, 2018).

3. Michael Cohen, "Hazard's Toll: The Cost of Inaction at the Salton
Sea" (2014), Pacific Institute, https://pacinst.org/publication/hazards
-toll (accessed June 15, 2018).

4. Elliot Spagat, "California approves rescue plan for shrinking Salton
Sea" (2017), Associated Press, www.apnews.com
/1aa1f946283a4457a613bbc3ad7d297a/California-approves-rescue
-plan-for-shrinking-Salton-Sea (accessed June 15, 2018).

5. Coachella Valley Water District, "Agricultural Irrigation and
Drainage," www.cvwd.org/166/Agricultural-Irrigation-Drainage
(accessed June 15, 2018).

6. John Lippert, "A Few California Farms Have Lots of Water. Can they Keep It?" (2015), www.bloomberg.com/features/2015-imperial -valley-water-barons (accessed June 15, 2018).

7. California Natural Resources Agency, "Salton Sea Management Program: Phase 1" (March 2017), http://resources.ca.gov/docs/salton _sea/ssmp-10-year-plan/SSMP-Phase-I-10-YR-Plan-with-appendices .pdf (accessed June 15, 2018).

8. Jim Steinberg, "California's new Salton Sea plan won't stop environmental disaster, Redlands expert says" (2017), www.redlandsdaily facts.com/2017/11/08/californias-modified-salton-sea-plan-wont -stop-environmental-disaster-redlands-expert-says (accessed June 15, 2018).

9. Gary Jennings and Dan Johnson, "Sea to Sea, importing seawater from Sea of Cortez to eliminate dust emissions from 75,000 acres at the Salton Sea and 150,000 acres at the Laguna Salada, BC Mexico" (2016), Jennings & Johnson Partnership, http://resources.ca.gov/docs /salton-sea/meetings-224/Jennings%20and%20Johnson%20Presentation .pdf (accessed June 15, 2018).

10. Michael Cohen, "Salton Sea Important/Export Plans," Pacific Institute, https://pacinst.org/publication/salton-sea-importexport -plans (accessed June 15, 2018).

11. Michael Cohen, "Salton Sea Important/Export Plans" Pacific Institute, https://pacinst.org/publication/salton-sea-importexport-plans (accessed June 15, 2018).

Map 03.02 Allocations on the Colorado

1. Donald Worster, quoting John Wesley Powell, "A river running west: reflections on John Wesley Powell," 2009, www.tandfonline .com/doi/full/10.1080/08873630903025055 (accessed August 20, 2018).

2. US Bureau of Reclamation, Law of the River: Colorado River Compact, 1922, www.usbr.gov/lc/region/g1000/pdffiles/crcompct.pdf (accessed June 15, 2018).

3. Dan Dubray, "Western Drought" (2018), US Bureau of Reclamation, www.usbr.gov/newsroom/presskit/factsheet/detail.cfm?recordid =13 (accessed June 15, 2018).

4. US Bureau of Reclamation, System Conservation Implementation Agreement (SCIA) between the United State Bureau of Reclamation and the Central Arizona Water Conservation District to Implement a Pilot System Conservation Program (Pilot Program) (2016), www.usbr .gov/lc/region/g4000/4200Rpts/DecreeRpt/2016/07.pdf (accessed June 15, 2018).

5. Brian Clark Howard, "Historic Pulse Flow Brings Water to Parched Colorado River Delta" (2014), *National Geographic*, https://news .nationalgeographic.com/news/2014/03/140322-colorado-river-delta -pulse-flow-morelos-dam-minute-319-water (accessed June 15, 2018).

6. US Bureau of Reclamation, Boulder Canyon Project Act, 1928, www.usbr.gov/lc/region/g1000/pdffiles/bcpact.pdf (accessed June 15, 2018).

7. US Bureau of Reclamation, Upper Colorado River Basin Compact, 1948, www.usbr.gov/lc/region/g1000/pdffiles/ucbsnact.pdf (accessed June 15, 2018).

8. US Department of the Interior, Drought in the Colorado River Basin (2014), www.doi.gov/water/owdi.cr.drought/en (accessed June 15, 2018).

9. Lori Pottinger, "The Search for Sustainability in the Colorado River" (2017), www.ppic.org/blog/search-sustainability-colorado -river-basin (accessed June 15, 2018).

10. Deborah Byrd, "Lake Mead reaches a new low" (2016), https://earthsky.org/earth/lake-mead-reaches-a-record-low-2016 (accessed June 15, 2018).

11. Grace Hood and Lauren Sommer, "High Demand, Low Supply: Colorado River Water Crisis Hits Across the West" (2016), National Public Radio, www.npr.org/2016/12/30/507569514/high-demand-low-supply-colorado-river-water-crisis-hits-across-the-west (accessed June 15, 2018).

PART FOUR: A MOMENT OF RESTORATION
Map 04.01 Hetch Hetchy Revisited

1. Sarah Null, "Time to Give a Dam: O'Shaughnessy Dam Is No Longer Needed," Sierra College, www.sierracollege.edu/ejournals/jsnhb/v6n1/null.html (accessed June 15, 2018).

2. Jessica Driver, "It's time to restore Hetch Hetchy" (2017), *California Aggie*, https://theaggie.org/2017/11/20/its-time-to-restore-hetch-hetchy (accessed June 15, 2018).

3. Jay Lund and Sarah Null, "Reassembling Hetch Hetchy: Water Supply without O'Shaughnessy Dam" (2006), *Journal of the American Water Resources Association*, https://watershed.ucdavis.edu/education/classes/files/content/page/Null-Lund_JAWRA_2007.pdf (accessed June 15, 2018).

4. Environmental Defense, "Tuolumne Watershed Diversions without Hetch Hetchy Reservoir: Comparison of Interties to Cherry and Don Pedro Reservoirs" (2005), https://d3n8a8pro7vhmx.cloudfront.net/hetchhetchy/pages/29/attachments/original/1410924131/edf_2005.pdf?1410924131.

5. Spreck Rosekrans, Nancy E. Ryan, Ann H. Hayden, et al., "Paradise Regained, Solutions for Restoring Yosemite's Hetch Hetchy Valley," Environmental Defense (2004) (XV) https://d3n8a8pro7vhmx.cloudfront.net/hetchhetchy/pages/29/attachments/original/1410924269/Paradise_Regained_2004.pdf?1410924269 (accessed June 15, 2018).

PART FIVE: PATTERNS IN CONSERVATION
05.b Agricultural Use, by the Numbers

1. University of California, Davis, "The Measure of California Agriculture," chapter 5, table 5.5 B, http://aic.ucdavis.edu/publications/moca/moca_current/moca09/moca09chapter5.pdf

2. California Department of Food and Agriculture, "Agricultural Land Loss and Conservation," www.cdfa.ca.gov/agvision/docs/Agricultural_Loss_and_Conservation.pdf.

3. California Department of Water Resources, "California Statewide Agricultural Land Use Mapping for Informed Decision Making and Temporal Change Assessment," 2017, www.grac.org/media/files/files/319db9f7/3.4_Kimmelshue_1_.pdf.

4. Federation of Associated Scientists, "California Agricultural Production and Irrigated Water Use," https://fas.org/sgp/crs/misc/R44093.pdf.

5. California Department of Water Resources, *California Water Plan*, 2013, www.drought.ca.gov/pdf/How-Water-Used-In-CA-Agricultural.pdf.

6. Pacific Institute infographic, in "Holy Cow! Crops That Use More Water Than Almonds," *TakePart*, www.takepart.com/article/2015/05/11/cows-not-almonds-are-biggest-water-users.

7. California Foundation for Agriculture, "Common Fact Sheet, Alfalfa," information compiled by the California Alfalfa and Forage Association, https://learnaboutag.org/resources/fact/alfalfa.pdf (accessed June 15, 2018).

8. David Pierson, "California farms lead the way in almond production" (2014), *Los Angeles Times*, www.latimes.com/business/la-fi-california-almonds-20140112-story.html (accessed June 15, 2018).

9. Keiller Kyle and Alex Hartman, "Farming for Birds: Alfalfa and forages as valuable wildlife habitat," 2010 California Alfalfa and Forage Symposium, University of California, Davis, and Audubon California, http://alfalfa.ucdavis.edu/+symposium/2010/files/talks/CAS07 _HartmanWildlifeHabitat.pdf (accessed June 15, 2018).

10. Maggie Monast, "Farmers open their books to show financial impact of conservation" (2018), Environmental Defense Fund, http:// blogs.edf.org/growingreturns/2018/04/17/conservation-farm-finance (accessed June 15, 2018).

11. California Department of Water Resources, California Irrigation Management System, https://cimis.water.ca.gov/ (accessed August 20, 2018).

12. California Department of Food & Agriculture, State Water Efficiency and Enhancement Program, www.cdfa.ca.gov/oefi/sweep (accessed August 20, 2018).

13. US Department of Agriculture, Irrigation Techniques, www.usda .gov/media/blog/2016/05/26/california-farmers-count-every-drop -efficient-irrigation-technologies (accessed August 20, 2018).

14. Heather Cooley, Peter Gleick, and Juliet Christian-Smith, "Sustaining California Agriculture in an Uncertain Future" (2009), Pacific Institute, www.pacinst.org.

05.c Urban Use, by the Numbers

1. David Carle, *Water and the California Dream* (Berkeley: Counterpoint, 2016), 106.

2. Los Angeles Department of Water & Power, Urban Water Management Plan (2010), 19, www.ladwp.com.

3. Dan Brekke, "19%: The Great Water-Power Wake-Up Call," www
.kqed.org/climatewatch/2012/06/10/19-percent-californias-great-water
-power-wake-up-call (accessed June 15, 2018).

4. Edward S. Spang et al., "The estimated impact of California's
urban water conservation mandate on electricity consumption and
greenhouse gas emissions," iopscience.iop.org/article/10.1088
/1748-9326/aa9b89 (accessed June 15, 2018).

5. Ellen Hanak and Jeffrey Mount, "Water Use in California," www
.ppic.org/publication/water-use-in-california (accessed June 15, 2018).

6. Pacific Institute, "Urban Water Conservation and Efficiency
Potential in California" (2011), 2, 4, www.pacinst.org/wp-content
/uploads/2014/06/ca-water-urban.pdf.

Western Osprey
Pandion haliaetus

7. CalRecycle, "Food Scraps Management: Organic Materials Management," www.calrecycle.ca.gov/organics/food (accessed August 20, 2018).

8. CalRecycle "Mandatory Commercial Organics Recycling," www.calrecycle.ca.gov/recycle/commercial/organics (accessed August 20, 2018).

05.d The Wisdom of Future Water Projects

1. There are other dam-raising options too, on the Shasta Dam, San Luis Reservoir, and Vaqueros Reservoir. See Adolph Rosekrans, "The Water Wars Around Us," Restore Hetch Hetchy, www.hetchhetchy.org/the_water_wars_around_us (accessed June 15, 2018).

2. Toward increased aridity and smaller intervals between drought occurrences, see: US Geological Society, California Water Science Center "Climate Change and Water Supply in California's Central Valley: A Model Approach" (2012), https://ca.water.usgs.gov/news/2012/ClimateChangeWaterSupplyCaCentralValley.html (accessed June 15, 2018).

3. These new projects all have billions of dollars on their price tags associated with water that may or may not come. Local system alternatives include water recycling and groundwater and rainwater collection; these are, across the board, more cost efficient. See Restore the Delta, *California's Sustainable Water Plan*, March 2017, "Conservation costs just $210 per acre-foot of water according to the Los Angeles County Economic Development Corporation. Compare that cost to new conveyance and surface storage water projects that cost between $760 to $2,000 per acre-foot of water." www.restorethedelta.org/californias-sustainable-water-plan-march-2017 (accessed June 15, 2018).

4. California Department of Water Resources, Bay-Delta Office, "California Central Valley Unimpaired Flow Data" (2007), www.waterboards.ca.gov/waterrights/water_issues/programs/bay_delta/bay_delta_plan/water_quality_control_planning/docs/sjrf_spprtinfo/dwr_2007a.pdf (accessed June 15, 2018).

5. Steve Patterson, Bita Ryan and Phil Helsel, "One year later, Oro-ville dam crisis still weighs on residents' minds" (February 2018), www.nbcnews.com/news/us-news/one-year-later-oroville-dam-crisis-still-weighs-residents-minds-n846021 (accessed August 20, 2018).

6. "Dr. Jeffrey Michael, Director of the Center for Business and Policy Research at the University of the Pacific, has pointed out that the investments in water conservation create 15 to 20 jobs per million dollars of expenditure." Restore the Delta, "California's Sustainable Water Plan March 2017," www.restorethedelta.org/californias-sustainable-water-plan-march-2017/ (accessed June 15, 2018).

7. American Rivers, "Restoring Damaged Rivers," www.american rivers.org/threats-solutions/restoring-damaged-rivers/dam-removal-map, Americanrivers.org (accessed June 15, 2018).

05.e Conservation Summary

1. An estimated 1.8 MAF of reservoir space is filled with silt; see George Skelton, "California's reservoirs are filled with gunk, and it's crowding out room to store water" (2017) *Los Angeles Times*, www.latimes.com/politics/la-pol-sac-skelton-silt-california-dams-20170306-story.html (accessed June 15, 2018).

2. George Skelton, "Does California really need more dams? We're running out of places to put them" (2017) Los Angeles Times, www.latimes.com/politics/la-pol-sac-skelton-california-water-capture-dams-20170220-story.html (accessed June 15, 2018).

3. Peter Gleik, "Is California Entering a Megadrought?" (2016) Pacific Institute, www.climateone.org/events/california-entering-megadrought (accessed June 15, 2018).

4. Carolyn Lochhead, "Dams remain in line for bulk of funding over cheaper alternatives," *San Francisco Chronicle*, www.sfchronicle.com/news/article/Dams-remain-in-line-for-bulk-of-funding-over-10946521.php (accessed June 15, 2018).

5. California Department of Water Resources "Making Water Conservation a California Way of Life," www.water.ca.gov/LegacyFiles /wateruseefficiency/conservation/docs/20170407_EO_B-37-16_Final _Report.pdf (accessed June 15, 2018).

6. US Geological Survey, "California Water Use, 2010," https:// ca.water.usgs.gov/water_use/2010-california-water-use.html (accessed June 15, 2018).

7. Pacific Institute, "Agricultural Water Conservation and Efficiency Potential in California," National Resources Defense Council, https:// pacinst.org/wp-content/uploads/2014/06/ca-water-ag-efficiency.pdf (accessed June 15, 2018).

8. Pacific Institute, "The Untapped Potential of California's Water Supply: Efficiency, Reuse, and Stormwater" (2014), https://pacinst.org /wp-content/uploads/2014/06/ca-water-capstone.pdf (accessed June 15, 2018).

9. Pacific Institute, "Urban Water Conservation and Efficiency Potential in California," National Resources Defense Council, https:// pacinst.org/wp-content/uploads/2014/06/ca-water-urban.pdf (accessed June 15, 2018).

Bibliography

Abbey, Edward. *Desert Solitaire*. New York: Ballantine, 1971.

Arax, Mark, and Rick Wartzman. *The King of California*. New York: Public Affairs, 2003.

Bakker, Elna S. *An Island Called California*. Berkeley: University of California, 1971.

Berry, Wendell. *The Unsettling of America*. San Francisco: Sierra Club, 1977.

Brower, David. *Let the Mountains Talk, Let the Rivers Run*. San Francisco: Harper, 1995.

Brower, Kenneth. *Hetch Hetchy: Undoing a Great American Mistake*. Berkeley: Heyday, 2013.

Carle, David. *Introduction to Water in California*. Berkeley: University of California Press, 2004.

Carle, David. *Water and the California Dream*. Berkeley: Counterpoint, 2016.

Childs, Craig. *The Secret Knowledge of Water*. New York: Back Bay Books, 2000.

Didion, Joan. *The White Album*. New York: Farrar, Straus and Giroux, 1979.

Farmer, Jared. *Trees in Paradise*. Berkeley: Heyday, 2017.

Kimmerer, Robin Wall. *Braiding Sweetgrass*. Minneapolis: Milkweed, 2013.

Kolbert, Elizabeth. *The Sixth Extinction*. New York: Picador, 2014.

McKibben, Bill. *The End of Nature*. New York: Anchor Books, 1989.

McPhee, John. *The Control of Nature*. New York: Farrar, Straus and Giroux, 1989.

Owen, David. *Where the Water Goes: Life and Death along the Colorado River*. New York: Riverhead, 2017.

Palmer, Tim. *Field Guide to California Rivers*. Berkeley: University of California Press, 2012.

Reisner, Marc. *Cadillac Desert: The American West and Its Disappearing Water*. New York: Penguin, 1986.

Rexroth, Kenneth. *In the Sierra*. New York: New Directions, 1981.

Snyder, Gary. *Mountains and Rivers Without End*. Berkeley: Counterpoint, 1996.

Stegner, Wallace. *The Sound of Mountain Water*. New York: Dutton, 1980.

Wallace, David Rains. *The Klamath Knot*. Berkeley: University of California Press, 2003.

Wilson, Edward O. *The Future of Life*. New York: Alfred A. Knopf, 2002.

Acknowledgments

I have been touring with the *California Field Atlas* for almost eight months and even more rewarding than presenting the work itself is the audience I become before this electric network of engaged citizens, a community ready for this nature-first narrative. I listen to the choir of neighbors ready to be counted in a nation that draws its strength from a healthy relationship with all systems of the natural world. Thank you to brilliant minds and supportive hearts that have invaluably assisted me and my work with this project and the *California Field Atlas*:

Mark Medeiros / Peninsula Open Space Trust
Matt Dolkas / Peninsula Open Space Trust
Victoria Schlesinger / *Bay Nature Magazine*
Brandy Dyess / Mojave Desert Land Trust
Robert Cushman / Friends of the River
Mark Dubois / Friends of the River
Mats Andersson / Indigofera Jeans
Michael Fried / Planet Earth Arts
Michael Dotson / Klamath Siskiyou Wildlands Center
Matt Decker / Premium Arts
Kristine Zeigler / Conservation International
Stephen Sparks / Point Reyes Books
Heather Hess / Truckee Bespoke
Sara Husby / Anza Borrego Foundation
Bob Schneider / Tuleyome
Ralph Lewin / Mechanics Institute of San Francisco
Malcolm Margolin / California Institute for Community, Art, and Nature
Lindsie Bear / Humboldt Area Foundation
Spreck Rosekrans / Restore Hetch Hetchy

Julene Freitas / Restore Hetch Hetchy
Janet Carle / Mono Lake Committee
Jake Sigg / California Native Plant Society
Robert Hall / California Native Plant Society
Mary Ellen Hannibal / Commonwealth Club of San Francisco
Ken Brower / Earth Island Institute
Hall Newbegin / Juniper Ridge
Lanny Kaufer / Herb Walks
Andrea Alday / Wilderness Society
Travis Longcore / Audubon Society
Marcos Trinidad / Audubon Society
Jason Mark / Sierra Club
Gary Snyder / writer
Laura Cunningham / artist
John Muir Laws / artist
Tom Killion / artist
Bryan Conant / Los Padres Forest Association
Jesse Carmichael / Biocitizen LA
Steve Wasserman / Heyday
Christopher Miya / Heyday
Diane Lee / Heyday
Ashley Ingram / Heyday
Gayle Wattawa / Heyday
Mariko Conner / Heyday
Emmerich Anklam / Heyday
Deborah Bruce-Hostler / copyeditor
Molly Woodward / proofreader
Jeffre Talltrees / Mom
Alli Darling / love
Gordy / dog

About the Author

What Obi Kaufmann is: a naturalist, a California native, an artist, a historian, a cartographer, sometimes a journalist.

What Obi Kaufmann is not: a scientist, a politician, a lobbyist, a lawyer, a farmer.

Obi Kaufmann is the author of the best-selling *California Field Atlas* and lives in Oakland.

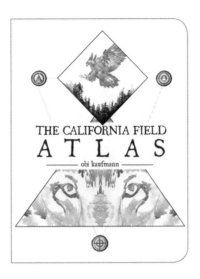

After the *California Field Atlas* was published in 2017, Kaufmann immediately went to work on another three field atlases. The forthcoming trilogy will tackle three generalized, provincial ecoregions within California: the forests, the coasts, and the deserts.

forests coasts deserts